Parent Pow...

Contributors

Nicholas Bagnall, education correspondent, *Sunday Telegraph*; former editor, *The Teacher*.

Peter Newell, former deputy editor, *Times Educational Supplement* and education officer, National Council for Civil Liberties; now working at White Lion Street Free School, Islington.

Michael Pollard, former teacher and educational editor; now freelance journalist.

Harry Rée, teacher; former professor of education, University of York.

Anna Sproule, freelance educational journalist.

Shirley Toulson, editor, *Child Education*.

Alison Truefitt, former education correspondent, *Evening Standard*; now working at White Lion Street Free School, Islington.

Nicholas Tucker, lecturer in psychology, University of Sussex.

Parent Power

*A Dictionary Guide to
your Child's Education and Schooling*

EDITED BY NICHOLAS BAGNALL

ROUTLEDGE & KEGAN PAUL
LONDON AND BOSTON

*First published in 1974
by Routledge & Kegan Paul Ltd
Broadway House, 68–74 Carter Lane
London EC4V 5EL and
9 Park Street,
Boston, Mass. 02108, USA
Set in Monotype Times
and printed in Great Britain by
The Camelot Press Ltd, Southampton*

© *Routledge & Kegan Paul Ltd 1974
No part of this book may be reproduced in
any form without permission from the
publisher, except for the quotation of brief
passages in criticism*

ISBN 0 7100 7944 3

Contents

Introduction	*page* vii	Department of	
In Loco Parentis	x	Education and Science	41
Absence	1	De-schooling	42
Accidents	2	Detention	42
Advice	3	Direct Grant Schools	43
Aptitude	5	Discipline	43
Art Schools	5	Discovery Methods	44
Assault	6	Drama	45
Assembly	8	Drugs	46
Attendance	9	Duke of Edinburgh's	
Backwardness	11	Award Scheme	47
Ballet	12	Dyslexia	47
Boarding Schools	13	Education Acts	49
Bullying	14	Educational Priority Areas	50
Careers	16	Educational Psychologists	50
Catchment Area	17	Educationally Subnormal	51
Certificate of Secondary		Eleven-plus	52
Education	18	Encyclopedias	53
Child Minders	19	Equipment	54
Choosing a School	19	Evening Classes	54
Church Schools	21	Examinations	55
Classes, Size of	22	Expulsion	58
Coaching and Cramming	23	Extras	59
Co-education	24	Family Grouping	61
Colleges of Education	25	Fees	61
Colleges of Further		Free Schools	62
Education	26	Games	63
Common Entrance	27	General Certificate of	
Community Schools	28	Education	64
Complaints	29	Gifted Children	65
Comprehensive Schools	31	Governors and Managers	66
Confidential Records	33	Grammar Schools	67
Confiscation and Fines	34	Grants	68
Corporal Punishment	34	Half-time Schooling	70
Correspondence Courses	35	Head Teacher	70
Counselling	36	Higher Education	71
Day Nurseries	37	Higher National Diploma	71
Deaf Children	37	HMC Schools	71
Degrees	38	Holidays	72
Delinquency	40	Home Education	73

vi *Contents*

Homework	76	Reading	103
Immigrants	77	Recognition as Efficient	105
Independent Schools	79	Registered Schools	105
Infant Schools	79	Religious Education	105
Inspectors	80	Reports	107
Integrated Day	80	Rules	108
Intelligence Tests	81	Scholastic Agencies	109
Junior Schools	82	School Councils	109
Leaving Age	83	School Fund	110
Libraries	83	School Journeys	110
Local Education		School Magazines	112
Authorities	84	Schools, Lists of	112
Maths	85	Secondary Schools	112
Medical Inspection	86	Secretary of State for	
Middle Schools	87	Education and Science	113
Milk and Meals	87	Sex Education	114
Music	88	Single-sex Schools	116
Nursery Schools and		Sixth-form Colleges	116
Classes	89	Smoking, Drinking	117
Open Plan	90	Special Schools	117
Open University	91	Speech Day	119
Ordinary National		Spelling	119
Certificate	91	Starting School	120
Ordinary National		State Schools	121
Diploma	91	Streaming	121
Parents' Rights	92	Subjects	123
Personal appearance	94	Teachers	123
Playgroups	95	Team-teaching	124
Politics	96	Textbooks	125
Polytechnics	97	Transport	125
Preparatory Schools	98	Truancy	126
Pressure Groups	99	Uniforms	127
Primary Schools	100	Universities	128
Progressive Schools	101	Welfare Benefits	130
Pupil Power	102		

Introduction

Legally, parents have very little power when it comes to the education of their children. The law tends to leave the final decisions to elected councillors on local education committees – or, through them, to the schools. The Department of Education and Science can seldom interfere, and even when it is allowed to, it often prefers to keep out of it.

In practice, though, parents have great power. Only in recent years have the experts begun to realize that the most important people in a child's education are not his teachers but his parents.

This book helps parents use that power.

In every case we explain their legal rights. But we also explain how in ordinary ways they can make use of the school system to the best advantage of their children.

We have avoided the lawyer's approach, for, as everyone knows, going to law is nearly always the worst way of solving a problem. What the law says, time and again, is that teachers and others should behave 'reasonably'. It's only when people stop behaving reasonably that the law needs to be called in. One way of putting it would be to say that this book helps you to make people see reason.

Obviously, a basic knowledge of the system is the first essential. Once parents know the system, they can begin to answer people in their own terms. They need no longer be pushed around.

They can begin to realize – for example – that teachers often have their own inferiority complexes, going right back to the days when the old School Boards used to treat them like dirt. Understandably, teachers want everyone to know that they are the professionals. Hence those warnings to parents not to interfere in their children's learning, not to question the rules of the school (however odd), not to come inside unless actually asked. If one knows why some teachers behave as they do, it's much easier to talk to them and to persuade them.

You realize, too, that local councillors may know a good deal less about children than you do, and that the education officials in County Hall are servants, not masters.

Here then, in quick-reference form, is the information you need if you want to see your child treated fairly and make sure that he (or she) is in the school (or college) that suits him best. There are also some suggestions for further reading.

We do not say what are the best schools. That would be begging the question of what schools are for. There is no general agreement on this question. Obviously some schools have quite different aims from others.

We do help the reader in finding out what the aims are, so that what the school wants *from* his children is the same as what he wants *for* them. That could be the most important thing of all.

Finally, a note on how to use the book. So many of the topics dealt with here overlap with each other that there's a danger of repetition. To avoid this, there is a simple system of cross-references. The entry on PARENTS' RIGHTS, for example, isn't by any means exhaustive, so the reader is directed to the other relevant entries in the book. We have tried to arrange things so that, whatever entry the reader starts from, by following the cross-references he can build up a fuller picture. The entry under ADVICE lists the main national organizations (and their addresses) which are of use to parents with education problems and is constantly referred to in other entries. It may be a good place to start from when using this book.

In Loco Parentis

The expression *in loco parentis* crops up many times in these pages, either directly or indirectly. It is the Latin for *in place of the parent* and refers to all schools, heads and teachers. It means that they have just the same rights in common law as parents have in the way they treat children. If you can beat your children, they can; if you can be had up for neglecting your kids, so can they. It applies only when a school or its teachers are actually in charge of the the children. It's a key phrase which assumes that the relationship between a child and his teachers is the same as that between a child and his parents. It's probably wrong, but it's the law.

Absence

Almost all schools expect some sort of note from you when your child has been absent. (It need only be a rough note – though remember these notes often get put into your child's CONFIDENTIAL SCHOOL RECORD.) They also like to have warning, especially where young children are concerned, if you plan to take your child out for the afternoon. Registers are, by law, taken at the start of each morning and afternoon. A search may be mounted for a child under nine, say, found unexpectedly missing after lunch.

What are 'legitimate' reasons for absence? You and the school may not agree on this. Illness, of course, the school will accept though too many 'coughs' and 'stomach aches' may arouse suspicion.

Family crises, too. Here the school will probably be more sympathetic than you expect. Teachers will be flattered if you take them into your confidence. They'll respond much more kindly to 'she's got to stay home to look after the baby, while I take my old mother to hospital', than to another 'cough'. Unless it happens too often.

Most schools will allow days off for special occasions – a brother returning from Australia, tickets for the Royal Tournament. If it's something your child wants to do very much, the school may agree that he is far more likely to learn something from it than from a resentful day's schooling.

Many schools allow older pupils to work at home during school-time, especially when they have to revise for exams. You may feel that your child would benefit from more time to work at home like this, and there would be no harm in your – or his – suggesting this to his teacher, or the head.

Some schools, especially since the school leaving age was raised to sixteen, have felt unable to offer suitable full-time activities for older pupils. They therefore let them go home 'unofficially' as it were, when there's nothing particularly useful laid on for them. This whole situation is bad for both pupils and school. If it affects your child, you might find the best thing was to see if the school will go so far as to allow him to take a job 'unofficially'.

Almost all children, at some point, detest the idea of going to

2   *Absence*

school. In some cases, this dread can be so deep and persistent that the school will accept it as a reason for absence, if it is confirmed by their psychologists. But don't be too quick to share their assumption that your child is suffering from some sort of mental illness (known as School Phobia). It is far more likely that he has a mature and sensitive reaction to a bad school.

If your child's absences are too frequent, or can't be explained in terms the school will accept, they will set the attendance machinery in motion (see ATTENDANCE).

It is likely that schools vastly overestimate the damage done, even to willing pupils, by long periods away from school – due to illness, for example. Children who have been off sick for whole terms seem to suffer surprisingly little in the long run. The social effects – having to remake friendships – could well matter more.

If a child is going to be away sick for more than a fortnight, but is well enough to get bored, the school may be willing – even anxious – to provide things for him to do, say by sending work through a classmate. There is a lot you can do yourself here (see HOME EDUCATION).

Accidents

It's as true in and around school as anywhere else that accidents will happen: occasionally on the way to and from school, in the classroom, during games and physical education periods, on school journeys and, most frequently of all, in the school playground.

The least helpful thing to do when accidents happen is to start making wild accusations of negligence or calling up solicitors. It's essential to find out exactly what happened and where it happened.

Local education authorities (in independent schools, the owners or governors) are responsible for accidents arising from the state of the school premises and its equipment – for example, a slippery floor or a rickety climbing-frame. Teachers are responsible for accidents which arise from their lessons, if they seem to have taken less than reasonable care. In situations where accidents are more likely – during break and the dinner-hour, for example – the school is responsible for providing supervision. Head teachers are bound by local authority rules to report accidents in some detail. Such reports provide a starting-point for any later inquiry.

Advice

Here are the names and addresses of the main national organizations able and anxious to help parents with problems:

Advisory Centre for Education (ACE), 32 Trumpington Street, Cambridge CB2 1QY. Publishes *Where* monthly. Subscribers can get personal advice for an extra fee. (Don't telephone.) Also runs a vocational guidance service. Details from the Centre to anyone who sends a stamped addressed envelope.

Campaign for Comprehensive Education, 1 Milland House, Alton Estate, London SW15. Publishes up-to-date reports on the movement towards comprehensive education.

Careers Research and Advisory Centre (CRAC), Bateman Street, Cambridge.

Child Poverty Action Group, 1 Macklin Street, London WC2.

Confederation for the Advancement of State Education (CASE), 81 Rustlings Road, Sheffield S11 7AB. Publishes bi-monthly *Parents and Schools* news sheets and *Parents and Schools Guidebook*, 1973. Has 100 local branches called Associations for the Advancement of State Education. Small subscription, varies between different associations.

Independent Schools Information Service, 34 Belgrave Road, Seaford, Sussex.

National Association of Governors and Managers, 34 Sandilands, Croydon, Surrey.

National Campaign for Nursery Education, Anlaby Lodge, Teddington, Middlesex.

National Children's Bureau, 8 Wakley Street, London EC1V 7QF. Publishes information on all aspects of children's growth and development, particularly disadvantaged children.

National Confederation of Parent–Teacher Associations, 1 White Avenue, Northfleet, Gravesend, Kent.

4   *Advice*

National Council for Civil Liberties, 186 King's Cross Road, London, WC1.

Pre-School Playgroups Association, Alford House, Aveline Street, London SE11.

For other specialized organizations see references at the bottom of the various entries in this book.

Further information: The Department of Education and Science, Elizabeth House, York Road, London SE1, issues a big range of four-page broadsheets called *Reports on Education*. Apply to the Department or to Her Majesty's Stationery Office for a list of them. The Department also has a series called *Trends in Education*, published every month, covering various educational topics in greater depth than the *Reports*. Councils and Education Press, 10 Queen Anne Street, London W1, publishes the *Education Committees Year Book* annually. More than 1,000 pages of close-printed names and addresses ranging from the biggest national organizations to your local secondary school head. From the same source, occasional *Digests* on particular topics. See also SCHOLASTIC AGENCIES.

Listed below are some general reference books. Numbers 1 and 4 are particularly good on modern teaching methods and how they've changed since earlier days. Numbers 5 and 10 are useful if your children are just starting school (but see what we say under READING). The rest are good on the workings of the education system generally. For something more detailed, there's Edward Blishen (ed.), *Blond's Encyclopaedia of Education*, Blond Educational, 1969, which is first-rate, although some of it is slightly out of date now.

1   David Ayerst, *Understanding Schools* (revised edn), Penguin, 1972.
2   E. B. Castle, *A Parent's Guide to Education*, Penguin, 1968.
3   Tyrrell Burgess, *A Guide to English Schools* (revised edn), Penguin, 1972.
4   Tyrrell Burgess, *Home and School*, Allen Lane, 1973.
5   Cynthia Mitchell, *Time for School*, Penguin, 1973.
6   Christopher Price (ed.), *Your Child and School* (3 vols: three to eight, nine to thirteen and fourteen to eighteen), Cornmarket Press, 1970.

7 Bruce Kemble, *Give Your Child a Chance*, Pan, 1972.
8 Michael Pollard, *Education Today and How it Works*, New English Library, 1970.
9 Central Office of Information, *Education in Britain*, HMSO, revised edn, 1971.
10 Brenda Thompson, *Learning to read; a Guide for Teachers and Parents*, Sidgwick & Jackson, 1970.
11 *Where on Parents and the Law*, ACE (see above).

Aptitude

Like INTELLIGENCE, aptitude is a rather vague word; it's generally taken to refer to ability in one particular field. Aptitude tests may try to measure skills as specific as musical or mechanical ability, whereas INTELLIGENCE TESTS always go for a more general assessment of a number of abilities.

In the 1944 Education Act it was laid down that the local authority had the duty to educate each pupil up to his age, ability and aptitude. But in fact local authorities have differed fairly widely since then on the amount of special provision they have been prepared to make. Some authorities have insisted that their own ordinary schools can perfectly well cater for all children whatever their aptitudes. Others have been more ready to grant scholarships to study somewhere else, or have set up their own specialized institutions.

Further information: P. E. Vernon, *The measurement of abilities*, University of London Press, 1956.

Art Schools

There are three main kinds of art school or college: (1) offering vocational courses of up to four years, in various specialized branches of art – printing, photography, industrial design, textile design and so forth; (2) offering, in addition to these, a foundation course leading to the Diploma in Art and Design; (3) the forty or so Dip AD colleges. A three-year course which automatically qualifies for a GRANT and is equivalent to a degree course in a university. Art schools may offer all these courses, or only the first two; or only the first.

Entry is by three or four GCE O-levels to the vocational courses, or by five O-levels to the others. But a person with exceptional talent might be able to get in on less, if his teacher recommends him. The schools are far more impressed by a good folder of work than by O-levels.

The vocational courses are OK for those who want to go into advertizing or into design agencies. Again, it's the work you've done that matters to employers more than a school's diploma.

The foundation course lasts either one year or two; it's a general course and helps a student decide what branch of art or design (and therefore which Dip AD college) he wants. But it's better to go for a two-year foundation course if possible. Applications for a Dip AD course have to be made only one-and-a-half terms after the start of the one-year course, which doesn't give much time to decide. Grants for the vocational or foundation courses are at the discretion of your local education authority.

The Dip AD colleges are fairly choosy about whom they will admit. A-levels are preferred, but a good folder is better still.

It's no good pretending that a Dip AD is any more of an instant passport to top jobs than is a university degree. The employment field is chronically restricted.

Further information: Art and Design, HMSO, 1971 (in the Choice of Careers series). *Directory of Design Courses*, Design Council, 28 Haymarket, London SW1Y 4S4.

Assault

This refers not only to teachers' assaults on pupils, but to pupils' assaults on teachers and occasionally on each other too.

First, assaults by teachers. Britain is among the few remaining countries of the developed world in which a wide range of physical assault on pupils is still a common and legal occurrence (see CORPORAL PUNISHMENT).

If you do feel that your child has been unreasonably hurt by a teacher, the first thing to do is to try and get the facts together and write them down. Of course if your child comes home hurt and upset, your first reaction may be to rush up to the school and try to sort it out there and then. But that may not be the best way of getting the facts. If the child is obviously hurt it is worth getting a doctor to examine him immediately.

Once you have got all the facts together you will want to decide what, if any, further action to take. If you decide that you want to make the school realize that you will not put up with this sort of treatment of your child, the best course is probably to make an appointment to see the teacher concerned and the head as soon as possible. Or write a letter.

If you decide this is not enough, you could go further and write to the parent-teacher association (see ADVICE), to the governors, or to the local education authority (see also COMPLAINTS). If you get no satisfaction out of any of these, and you feel that the local authority is acting unreasonably in refusing to take any action on your complaint, you can appeal direct to the Secretary of State for Education.

You may feel that the incident is serious enough to consider taking legal action. Remember that this will cost money. So find out if you qualify for legal aid or can use a free legal advice centre. A teacher who exceeds his authority and punishes unreasonably lays himself open to two kinds of prosecution – criminal proceedings by the Director of Public Prosecutions, and private proceedings by the parent on behalf of the child. If you decide to report the incident to the police they will want to investigate it fully for themselves, and will then decide whether or not to go ahead with a prosecution. A solicitor will advise you on whether it is worthwhile launching a private prosecution. Be warned: the courts tend to protect the authority of the teacher.

One kind of assault by teachers on which the law so far in Britain is absolutely ruthless is sexual assault. The law here is that which applies to all sexual relations – there is no special law relating to schools.

A technical 'assault' may not be harmful. But if you feel that your child has been seriously upset by a sexual assault, the first steps are the same as for non-sexual assault. However, remember that some young children are more upset by the interrogation and cross examination that go with a court case than by the original assault itself!

As for assault by a pupil on a teacher or on another pupil, if your child is involved you may be asked to see the head. In this case you must also try to find out all the facts.

If there is any suggestion that your child may be the subject of either civil or criminal proceedings, it is most unwise for him to allow himself to be interviewed or make any statements without taking legal advice: the Judges' Rules indicate that wherever practicable, if a child is interviewed by the police it should be in the presence of a parent or guardian – or, failing that, another person who is not a police officer should be present who is of the same sex as the child. In practice, you would be well advised only to allow an interview in the presence of a solicitor. The rules say that a parent or child is entitled to telephone a solicitor or friend provided this causes no hindrance to the administration of justice. See also BULLYING.

Assembly

Section 25 of the 1944 Education Act lays down that 'the school day . . . shall begin with collective worship on the part of all pupils in attendance'. However, all parents have the right to demand that their children be excused. This means that the children will be sent, at the time of assembly, to sit with those others whose parents have various religious faiths – or none. Usually they'll wait, under supervision, in a classroom. This is a good chance to polish off homework.

Assembly is supposed to create a sense of unity, and it can be an outward sign of that unity, where this exists. But in a school where there is conflict and dissension, it is at best a joke, at worst an embarrassing act of hypocrisy.

In a primary school, assembly can mean much to little children (and to their teachers). For seven-year-olds, to be one of a large group singing or reciting in unison can be a very enjoyable experience. By the age of seventeen, for most participants it's a bore; and this goes for staff too, who at least don't have to attend, unless they want to hear the notices. But assembly may still be of great importance for the head. For a few moments each day he feels himself in control of his school, whether he's saying the Lord's Prayer, reminding the children of some current disaster the other side of the world, or slating them for their disgraceful behaviour on the buses.

In very large schools, 'collective worship' is a mere shadow of the idea which once brought the whole school community together to 'worship the Lord'. Lack of space has made 'form prayers' in some schools a necessity, perhaps devised and taken by pupils; sometimes there are 'house assemblies' taken by the house tutor. For many pupils, on some days of the week, there may be no collective worship at all, even though they've not asked to be excused.

This may be against the law. But until the 1960s there was an act on the statute book which said that all those not going to church on Sunday would be fined a shilling!

Attendance

State schools have to be open for about 200 days a year. The law defines it as 400 sessions – a session being a morning or an afternoon – from which up to twenty may be deducted for occasional holidays (see *Schools Regulations 1959*, below). It's assumed that when the school is open the children must be there – with the exception of the annual two-week holiday allowance described under HOLIDAYS.

What happens if they aren't there?

The child's absence is noted not only in the register (taken by law at the start of each morning and afternoon) but also, in most areas, in a special absence book. This has a page for each child so that any pattern of absences, or accumulation of absences, can be clearly seen.

These books are inspected every week or so by the education welfare officers for the school – formerly known as truancy officers or School Board Men.

If they decide your child has been absent for too long, or for no 'good' reason, in their view, then they may write to you or visit you. Sometimes, the first few such letters may come from your child's class teacher who will hand the case over to the EWOs only if it looks like being 'difficult'.

10   Attendance

How long your child must be away before some action is taken varies enormously from area to area and school to school. In tough areas of large cities it may be six weeks or more before anything is done. And the older they are – and (in some cases) the more of a nuisance they are when in school – the less urgency is felt about them. There are undoubtedly a number of children whose truancy is tacitly accepted by the schools.

In country and suburban areas, and in primary schools, action may follow after a week's absence or even less.

To begin with the EWO will probably visit you to try to find a clear-cut reason for the child's absence, and then will try and suggest ways round it. Most are sympathetic at this stage.

If the problem is not immediately solved, the LOCAL EDUCATION AUTHORITY will warn parents that they are liable to fine and imprisonment (maximum £10 the first time and £20 and/or a maximum of one month in prison for second or subsequent offences).

If this doesn't have the desired effect, the EWOs' visits may become less friendly, and the LEA will serve an official 'attendance order' on the parents. These orders set a time limit by which the child must be in school, and name the school which the LEA expects the child to attend. The parents can object to the school chosen, and name another.

If you are keeping your child out of school because you object to the one named in the attendance order, this is where your legal fight begins. There are various grounds on which your objection may have to be met by the LEA. In the last resort the Secretary of State can arbitrate (see CHOOSING A SCHOOL and PARENTS' RIGHTS).

Most LEAs are extremely reluctant to take parents to court. They will go on visiting, arranging meetings and trying to persuade parents for perhaps a year or more.

The first prosecution is likely to be for simply breaking the attendance law – for which the fine can be as low as £1. If this doesn't work, the LEA may then ask the court to remove the child from the care of the parents, on grounds that the parent is 'not a fit person' to be in charge of the child if he can't get him to school regularly or is not educating him at home.

If the court agrees then the child is taken 'into care' of the local authority, and probably put in a day or boarding children's home. The length of such a 'care order' is decided by the court.

If the cause of a child's absence is thought to be some real difficulty at school or 'dread' of school, then you and the child will be asked to see the EDUCATIONAL PSYCHOLOGIST. If they agree that there is a problem of this kind, then it is up to the LEA to make suitable arrangements to help the child, and you, meanwhile, cannot be prosecuted for his non-attendance.

Further information: The Schools Regulations 1959 (Statutory Instruments 1959 No. 364: Education England and Wales), HMSO, 1959. *The Schools (Amending) Regulations 1966* (no. 1572: Local Government England and Wales), HMSO, 1966.

Backwardness

Children described as 'retarded', 'slow learners' or 'late developers' cannot keep up with other children of the same age in school subjects, especially in reading and arithmetic. They may be so backward as to be officially classified as EDUCATIONALLY SUBNORMAL (ESN), and sent to a special school. But usually they will be left in the ordinary school, and simply withdrawn from class at some stage during the day to work with a teacher specially trained in remedial work.

Some large secondary schools organize groups of backward children into small classes, because it is thought that the children will get on better if they work with one teacher for most of the time, and can have the advantage of a small class. The aim of any teacher working with a backward child is to help him to rejoin the ordinary classes as soon as possible.

If your child is found to be in need of remedial teaching you should have an opportunity to talk it over with his head teacher, his class teacher, the remedial teacher, and even possibly the EDUCATIONAL PSYCHOLOGIST. It is not usually advisable to try and cram him with a lot of extra work at home in a desperate attempt to get him to catch up. Nor is it wise to make private coaching arrangements with a teacher, either from the child's school or outside.

If you think your child may be backward, and haven't been

officially told so by his class teacher or head teacher, then you should discuss the matter with them.

Backwardness usually has more to do with emotional disabilities than with mental ones. Backward children may have 'learning blocks' which handicap them in one branch of learning – say mathematics – though they may be quite all right in other things.

Closely connected with backwardness is 'under-achievement'. The child doesn't work as well as you'd expect him to. Children like this used to be called lazy, but that is a word which doesn't usually help put matters right.

A lazy child or one who is constantly under-achieving is showing by his behaviour that something is wrong. It could be his emotional development, or it could be his relations with people at school or at home. The only way to solve his problem is to talk openly about it with his teachers.

Further information: C. Burt, *The Backward Child* (3rd edn), London University Press, 1950.
Useful organization: British Association for the Retarded (BAR), 17 Pembridge Square, London W2 4EP.

Ballet
Training for ballet should start preferably at nine and not later than eleven. Fees are not small. Whether you can cover them with a grant depends on the generosity of your local education authority.

Further information: Royal Academy of Dancing, 251 Knightsbridge, London SW7 10G. Royal Ballet School, 155 Talgarth Road, Barons Court, London W14 9DE.

Banding. See STREAMING.

Blind Pupils. See SPECIAL SCHOOLS.

Boarding Schools

There are two kinds of boarding: free, and heavily paid-for. In certain circumstances, local education authorities will pay for a child to go to an independent boarding school, or send him to a state boarding school or to the boarding section of a state day school, if they have one.

What circumstances? There is no hard-and-fast rule about this, but there are four basic categories that will get a sympathetic hearing at your local education offices. These are cases where: (1) both parents are abroad; (2) parents live in Britain but are likely to move house once every year or two; (3) home circumstances risk causing serious harm to a child's development; and (4) a special ability shown by the child requires special training only available at a boarding school.

An absent or deceased parent (especially the mother); severe or chronic parental ill-health (mental as well as physical); difficulties between parents likely to distress a child ('parental incompatibility'); bad housing conditions: all these are possible grounds for claiming a free boarding place.

The attitudes shown by different LEAs to the question vary. But if you feel your child would benefit from a boarding education, and if you can back your case with at least one of the reasons outlined above, it's worth seeing what your LEA can do. There's no difficulty about applying – just apply.

If you can't get help from there, you have to ask: Can I afford a fee-paying boarding school? (see FEES). Is it worth it?

Points against: Most boarding schools are still single-sex; boarding cuts children both off from their parents and the 'real' world; it limits a child's chance to organize his own life; and condemns misfits to months of suffering, unrelieved until the holidays come; there are still some schools where homosexuality and brutality can be found. The only way to find out is through friends and their children who know the school.

Most independent boarding schools have a traditional curriculum of academic work leading to GCE, which may not suit your child. There are some good non-academic ones, but they are harder to find.

Points in favour: Most boarding school pupils enjoy living with their own age-group; they may get better facilities for work and play at school than they might at home; they are taught in smaller classes, at least in the good schools; more and more boarding schools allow weekly boarding: pupils go home at week-ends.

However much you yourself may believe in boarding education, a critical eye is still important when you actually choose a boarding school. Work out what you want from it and what your child is likely to want from it.

Further information: The Independent Schools Information Service (see ADVICE), publishes helpful pamphlets, gives advice, and lists independent schools. It is run by the independent schools themselves. Royston Lambert, *The Hothouse Society*, Weidenfeld & Nicolson, 1968 and Penguin, 1974, includes confidential diaries of boarding school pupils, shows how bad some schools can be. Royston Lambert, *The State and Boarding Education: a factual report*, Methuen, 1966. For more information see also SCHOOLS, LISTS OF; CO-EDUCATION; SINGLE-SEX SCHOOLS; HMC SCHOOLS.

Bullying

Most children have felt 'picked on' at some time or another, and parents should certainly resist the urge to complain at the first grumble. What may seem like bullying to one child may be boisterous play to another; one of those things one just has to learn to cope with, given enough sympathy and support at home. But if a parent suspects consistent bullying, whether the children mention it or not, then of course something should be done, particularly if the child in question has become depressed or started to dread school.

If the teacher, on inquiry, denies any bullying, this needn't always be conclusive. So much of this can happen on the playground or around the lavatories, where no teacher may be directly involved. Better, therefore, to ask the school to keep a particular watch for the next few days and then have another meeting. Obviously it is best in any such interview to keep calm. Schools may feel and act rather defensively if you are over-determined to have a show-down.

If it turns out that your child has been largely imagining the bullying, then this will still be worth following up, as it may hint at a more general difficulty in getting on with other children. But what if you find for certain that bullying has taken place? Increasing watchfulness by all concerned may do a great deal to stop it, particularly where bullying has to a certain extent become organized without the teachers knowing it, as in some school 'protection rackets' operating in the playground or after school. In more isolated cases the solution may be harder; some children seem to have an urge to bully, despite punishment, possibly because they despise in others weaknesses they suspect to be in themselves: fearfulness, for example, or unpopularity. And then there are other children who appear almost to tempt bullying, perhaps because of the attention they get in this way; they're forever putting themselves in the way of trouble, and almost missing the bully when he is away from school. Here, each type of child may need some other sort of assistance, and the EDUCATIONAL PSYCHOLOGIST may be able to suggest help.

And what if the bully is a teacher? Again, a great deal of discretion and double-checking is called for before taking any action. But undeniably some teachers can become very irritable with a few, particular children, sometimes with reason, sometimes perhaps not. A meeting between the parent and the teacher, perhaps apparently to discuss the child's progress but in fact to try to take some of the heat out of the situation, can often help. If this fails, and the problem seems likely to persist, then the parent would be advised to see the head teacher with a view to changing the child's class.

Finally, how can you tell whether your own child is a bully? Not easy – you can only look for the obvious clues: seeing him bash smaller children on more than one or two occasions, seeing him in company with children who are known bullies, or, of course, getting complaints from teachers or other parents.

Bullies may need help just as much as people who are being bullied.

Further information: **D. H. Stott,** *The Social Adjustment of Children,* University of London Press, 1958.

16   *Careers*

Caning. See CORPORAL PUNISHMENT.

Careers

It may be necessary to turn your attention to careers much earlier than you think, especially if your son or daughter is going to take GCE or CSE. Employers may ask for particular subjects. It may be absurd to have to make even tentative decisions at the age of fourteen, the age for choosing what O-levels to take. But it is worse to plump for a particular career at sixteen or later only to find you haven't the right O-level subjects.

The system of advising school leavers on future jobs is less than perfect. The two obvious sources of information, the schools and the Careers Service, both have their weaknesses, and it's advisable to supplement what they offer with as much information as you can find.

Schools first, though. If your child is lucky, he'll be able to call on the service of a full-time careers teacher who will know – or know where to find out about – the entire business: job openings, the qualifications needed, where to apply, and the subjects a pupil will need to study. Since he is a teacher, he will also know about the children themselves. He may not be so good on careers for the non-academic child.

Unfortunately the full-time careers teacher is a rare bird. More usually, a careers teacher is an ordinary member of staff who fits his advisory work in with his other teaching commitments, and has neither time nor opportunity to gather all the information his pupils need.

It's here that the Careers Service helps to fill the gap. Working in conjunction with schools, it provides information on employment and careers, gives vocational guidance, helps to find job openings, and also continues to advise youngsters once they have started working.

Included in the service is an interview by the local careers officer with every school leaver who wants it; and remember that parents can be present if they wish. Follow-up meetings can also be arranged.

The Service is meant to supplement, not compete with, the

school's careers work; but, even so, not all teachers are happy with it. Their argument is that it can be too divorced from the school.

Now for the outside sources of help. One kind is computer assessment firms: the firms which put all the necessary information about the person into a computer, and hey presto, out comes the right career. That's the idea, anyway. Some charge quite a lot for this. For less personalized but much cheaper information, keep an eye on the careers sections run by various magazines and national newspapers.

For general advice there is, too, the non-profit making Cambridge organization called the Careers Research and Advisory Centre, 12 Bateman Street, Cambridge. This, in addition to its training work for careers advisers, produces a mass of publications that can be used in or out of school.

ACE (see ADVICE) has a careers advisory service and a vocational guidance service.

Further information: CRAC, *Your Choice* series: *Your choice at 14-plus; Your choice at 16-plus; Your choice at 18-plus; Your choice beyond a degree.* (A list of other publications is available.) Ruth Miller, *Careers for girls*, Penguin, 1970. C. Avent and E. L. Fried, *Starting Work*, Max Parrish, 1965. C. Avent, *Which Career?* Hale, 1970. Central Youth Employment Executive, Choice of Careers series pamphlets, HMSO. *Education and training*, Macmillan (monthly journal with careers section). Central Youth Employment Council, *Careers Guide*, HMSO, annually.

Catchment Area

However much parental freedom of choice might be built into the education system (see EDUCATION ACTS) it would never be physically possible to let every child go to the school of the parents' choice. Local authorities define 'catchment areas' for their schools, naming the streets or roads from which each school takes its pupils. This procedure is sometimes called 'zoning'. The head of a zoned school will usually tell parents what his area is. Otherwise the information can be got from the local education office.

Local authorities must operate zoning with 'reasonable consideration for the wishes of parents', and this means that catchment areas are not absolutely watertight. But if you want to cut across them you have to have good reasons, not merely personal preferences or local gossip about which school is best.

Religious denominational preferences (see CHURCH SCHOOLS) are usually regarded as good reasons for breaking the zoning rule. Possible danger from traffic on the way to or from school is another reason often given sympathetic consideration – provided it's genuine. But if you really feel strongly that you'd prefer your child to go to one particular school rather than another, it's always worth trying; nothing can be lost. See also CHOOSING A SCHOOL.

Certificate of Secondary Education (CSE)

A nationally recognized exam taken normally at sixteen, by pupils not thought to be up to the GCE. There are five grades: (1) Equivalent to a GCE O-level pass; (2) considerably above average; (3) a little above the average for sixteen-year-olds as a whole; (4) average; (5) this would not normally qualify for the Certificate, but the school and the candidate is told about it. The CSE has three 'Modes' or kinds of exam: (1) Papers set and marked outside the school; (2) papers marked outside the school, but specially set for that school; (3) papers set and marked inside the school (see EXAMINATIONS).

The CSE is useful for school leavers because it has now been recognized by employers. (It's been in existence only since 1965.)

It's supposed to be too hard for pupils in the bottom 40 per cent of ability. But plenty such pupils do succeed in it. Also plenty take it who are well up to the GCE. In some ways it's a more interesting exam as it usually needs less cramming.

Attempts are now being made to combine CSE and O-level in a single examination.

Further information: A Common System of Examining at 16-plus, Schools Council Examinations Bulletin no. 23, Evans/Methuen Educational, 1971. For quite a good account of the CSE, there's the Department of Education's *Reports on Education No. 47, The Certificate of Secondary Education*, HMSO, June 1968.

Child Minders

If you have to go out to work, and have no close friend or relative living nearby to look after your child, you will probably have to leave him with a child minder, for it is not often easy to find a place in a DAY NURSERY. A child minder is a woman who takes children who are not related to her, into her home to look after them. By law she must be registered at the Town Hall or Council House, so that her premises can be inspected to make sure that they are safe and adequate to the needs of young children. Do not leave your child with anybody who is not properly registered. The risks are too great.

The best way to set about finding a reliable child minder is to ask one of the Health Visitors at your local infants' and toddlers' clinic. Fees for child-minding are a matter of private arrangement between the minder and the mother, so it is not possible to quote an exact figure, but it can run to over £6 a week.

Further information: Nurseries and Child Minders Regulation Act 1948, HMSO. Sonia Jackson, *The Illegal Child-Minders*, Association of Multiracial Playgroups, 1971.

Choosing a school

There are good reasons for parents being choosy about which school their children go to; and you don't necessarily have to pay fees to be selective.

Prospective fee-payers can become bewildered by the range of choices. Your best policy in the first instance is to write to one of the SCHOLASTIC AGENCIES for a list of possible schools which will suit your purse and purposes, and then start writing. See also INDEPENDENT SCHOOLS, HMC SCHOOLS and BOARDING SCHOOLS for more advice.

If you're going to stay within the state system, write to your local chief education officer for a list of the schools available for your child.

How much choice can you in fact expect?

Local authorities often can't offer any choice at all of primary school. They want to encourage parents to use the school nearest their home. But even in these circumstances it's worth testing the possibility of choice.

With secondary schools, alternatives are not uncommon, although no parents can be guaranteed to get their first choice. Religious conviction can help you to a place in a 'voluntary' school; an elder brother or sister at one school may help a sister or a brother get there. In the end, if it comes to a tussle, the local education authority nearly always wins (see PARENTS' RIGHTS). But, whatever the odds, it's worth trying to exercise choice based on broad educational preference. Not only do you get more satisfaction from something you've chosen for your child, but the child, too, is given positive evidence that you care and the school justifiably gains in self-esteem when it's been chosen rather than just accepted (see CATCHMENT AREA).

The first thing to do is to write to the head, or telephone the school secretary, and ask for an appointment – and for a prospectus if they have one. Many people find they need to steel themselves a little when entering a head's study, but this can be overcome if you remind yourself that a head is, in fact, your paid employee (like a judge or a policeman); if it's an independent school the reminder is hardly necessary, and you can look on the head as a salesman, who wants your custom.

If the head says he can't see prospective parents, write to the chief education officer and complain. If the chief education officer tries to discourage you, ask him for the name of the chairman of the GOVERNORS OR MANAGERS. This could well unlock the door for you, unless by that time you've lost all interest in a school which is so uninterested in you.

Try to visit the school while the pupils are there – or if your appointment is 'after school', try and get there early, and watch the way the children (and the staff) leave the building. If a lot of them linger, this almost certainly is a good sign. Look at them, children and staff, in the playground. Talk, if you can, to other parents with children in the school. In the infants' department this is easy, as they'll be at the school gate. But beware of taking evidence from one mother only – she may be sour, or a favourite of the head's.

When you get inside, look at the notice boards if you can, to get an idea of the activities encouraged by the school. And then talk with the head; or it it's a very big school indeed, you may have to put up with a head of a house – this is not unreasonable.

Many of the entries in this dictionary could provide you with a check-list for your questions. Bear in mind that this first interview is a good opportunity to start a friendly relationship with the school, so the appearance of being pleasantly surprised by what you learn about the school may actually help your child. And so will a genuine concern for his future, and this is why it's important to take trouble over choosing a school.

Further information: Choosing a School, ACE (see ADVICE), 1974.

Church Schools

Church schools (also called voluntary schools) are those founded by the religious denominations, and originally they taught the faith and worship of their own Churches, but this is no longer necessarily so. Many have given up this privilege in exchange for more money from the state. Well over half the Church of England schools have done this.

A 'voluntary controlled' school must not give denominational instruction, must not hold denominational worship. A 'voluntary aided' school is allowed to give its own kind of religious teaching and worship. Practically all Roman Catholic schools are voluntary aided.

Unlike controlled schools, which are hardly different from ordinary state schools, the governors and managers of aided schools can have quite an influence on the teaching in them, largely through the appointment of their teachers. Other things being equal, a Church parent would have a prior claim to a place in one.

Non-Church parents can withdraw their children from the religious lessons and the denominational assembly (see RELIGIOUS EDUCATION). Apart from that, you just have to consider whether you want a school whose governors and teachers believe in a faith you don't necessarily believe in yourself.

The huge majority of Church of England aided schools are primary schools and you may not have any choice in your neighbourhood.

Further information: For information about Church of England schools, write to the National Society for Promoting Religious Education, 69 Great Peter Street, London, SW1. For information about Catholic schools, the Catholic Education Council, 47 Cromwell Road, London SW7 2DJ.

Classes, Size of

There's nothing in the regulations to say how large or small a class should be. The only rule is that classes should be 'not overcrowded' – whatever that may mean.

Nowadays we are asked to think in terms of pupil–teacher ratios. The idea is that with modern, flexible methods some classes could quite well be over forty whereas others might be too big at twenty. In schools which use TEAM-TEACHING absolute numbers don't mean so much; people think in groups, which change according to what the pupils are doing rather than in terms of fixed, box-type units called 'classes' (see also INTEGRATED DAY).

Some schools these days, particularly primary schools, are designed as OPEN PLAN schools to allow for this sort of arrangement. However, the odds are at present that your child won't be in an open plan school.

You may have reason to feel aggrieved if you find that yours is in a huge class while classes elsewhere in the school are thin on the ground. Unless there's been a big influx of children into the younger classes lately, it could mean the head isn't using his staff properly.

Clothing Allowance. See UNIFORMS.

Coaching and Cramming

The words 'coaching' and 'cramming' tend to be used rather loosely: often the first is just a polite word for the second. But by coaching we really ought to mean the extra help given outside the usual timetable to give the child a chance to catch up. Some schools will arrange this if the child has fallen behind in a particular subject, say because of illness or bad teaching earlier. It's a question of finding someone who is willing to do it. Fee-paying schools are often happy to see to it with (you guessed it) an extra charge. The practice of teachers accepting fees for coaching their own pupils is officially condemned by the National Union of Teachers.

Coaching for the ELEVEN-PLUS is a different matter. There are primary schools which positively discourage it because they think it gives unfair advantages. The answer is, of course, that a good primary school should give all its children a bit of coaching in the techniques needed to answer eleven-plus-type questions, so long as they don't get obsessed by it. It needs only a few sessions anyway; beyond that, there's not much point in it.

But you should think very carefully before arranging private coaching for the eleven-plus. Children have been gravely damaged by ambitious parents mad to get them into a grammar school where they can't cope with the work once they've got there, or they feel extra guilty if they can't get there after all.

Don't judge a primary school merely by its eleven-plus results.

Cramming means that a child is pumping himself full of facts (with or without help from teachers, tutors, parents, or bad little textbooks produced for the purpose) which he needs in order to pass an exam. He may pass all right, but he's no wiser about the subject. Some very efficient cramming is done by some of the minor public schools, to say nothing of the less good independent schools in general.

The only time cramming is justified is when a pupil has to get a paper qualification in a subject he's not going to take any further. For instance, a university history department might insist on O-level Latin, though the pupil might be a rotten Latinist yet a good potential historian.

Again, some exam syllabuses are so poor and irrelevant that

they positively encourage cramming. They deserve to be crammed for. Here one can only sigh over the waste of time involved.

There are various private coaching establishments or tutorial colleges (colloquially called crammers) for those who want them; not all are bad. Many are for A-level or Oxford or Cambridge entrance examinations. Others offer O-level courses.

Further information: From the SCHOLASTIC AGENCIES. ACE (see ADVICE) also publishes a list.

Co-education

This is the system of educating boys and girls in the same school. Parents' preferences for mixed or single-sex schools are very often taken into account by local authorities (see CHOOSING A SCHOOL). But this is less often possible than it used to be; in some places local authorities have combined boys' and girls' secondary schools to form comprehensive schools. More boys' independent schools are also beginning to take in girls, though usually on a small scale. Co-education is less common in boarding than in day schools.

There are two main arguments in favour of co-education: one social, one educational. On the social side, there is the claim that boys and girls who have learnt to get along with each other through childhood and adolescence find it easier to make tension-free relationships in later life.

If the two sexes are cooped up separately during their school years, the supporters of co-education go on, they will be awkward, shy and insecure in each other's presence – and this awkwardness will take several years to vanish entirely, if indeed it ever does.

On the educational side, academic experience abroad has shown that co-education works just as well, if not better, than the single-sex system.

For the argument *against* the co-ed system, see SINGLE-SEX SCHOOLS.

Further information: R. R. Dale, *Mixed or Single-sex School?*

(3 vols.), Routledge & Kegan Paul, 1965, 1967 and 1974. J. W. B. Douglas, J. M. Ross and H. R. Simpson, *All Our Future*, Panther, 1971. See also SCHOOLS, LISTS OF.

Colleges of Education

These used to be called Teacher Training Colleges, and until recently this phrase explained what they were. They still prepare students for the teaching certificate, but soon most of them will offer other qualifications as well, which don't necessarily lead to teaching. The certificate course lasts three years and includes supervised teaching practice in schools. The minimum entry requirements for this course is still five O-levels in the GCE, but most students today have at least one A-level.

The most important new course leads, after two years, to a Diploma in Higher Education (Dip HE). Students who do well enough in their Diploma course can stay on for one or two years and be awarded either a degree and/or a teaching certificate, depending on the subjects studied, and on whether their course has included teaching practice. The students normally choose the subjects they study. Minimum entry requirement for the Dip HE is the same as for any degree course anywhere – five GCE passes, two of them at A-level.

One year post-graduate courses are also offered by the colleges. These are for graduates from universities or polytechnics who want to teach, who need to be trained, and for whom a teaching certificate is essential.

The colleges have gone through a turmoil of change in the past ten years. They are now becoming accepted, alongside the universities and polytechnics, as equal partners offering a not dissimilar, but a characteristic course in higher education.

Further information: The Central Register and Clearing House, 3 Crawford Place, London W1H 2BN, deals with all applications to colleges of education, and publishes a list of colleges in *Summary of Teacher Training Colleges at Colleges and Departments of Education*, annually. Margaret Miles, *And Gladly Teach*, Educational Explorers, Reading, 1966, gives a clear picture of what teaching (and teacher training) is like. *Teacher Education and Training* (James Report), HMSO, 1972, for detailed background; it led to the changes described above.

Colleges of Further Education

Further education is officially defined as 'full-time and part-time education for persons over compulsory school age', but it doesn't mean education in universities or other places for degree-level work, which is called 'higher education'.

'FE colleges' may also be called technical colleges, technical institutes, municipal colleges, or just 'techs'. Or colleges of technology; but there's a difference here, see below.

All these are run by local education authorities. So you could say the techs start where the schools leave off. But actually they overlap. Courses offered by a technical college include those leading to O- and A-levels. Teenagers fed up with the restrictions of school life, to say nothing of its compulsory religion, assemblies and games, can switch to the more adult surroundings of the tech. Also, if you're in a good area, the school will let a pupil take subjects in the tech which it can't provide itself. He'll need to be strong-minded to keep up with the homework. For the over-eighteens, you may expect to have to pay a nominal fee.

What the technical colleges are mainly known for, however, is the scope of the vocational courses they offer. Students there can be trained in a very wide variety of skills connected with industry, commerce, and other fields of employment. The colleges have close links with industry, and can put on any course for which there is a demand.

A lot of the work at a technical college is done on a part-time basis, and a lot of tech students may already be in employment.

The level of courses run by the colleges of further education is in general lower than that found in the colleges of technology. FE colleges do work leading to craft and technical qualifications like the Ordinary National Certificate or Diploma, the City and Guilds certificate, and the Royal Society of Arts qualifications.

The colleges of technology offer the more advanced studies: courses leading to the Higher National Diploma, the Higher

National Certificate, and – occasionally – degrees. Qualifications for college entry depend very much on the colleges themselves, and on the type of course. For information, get in touch with the further education officer at your local education office.

For more information still, contact one of the ten regional bodies that deal with further education. They are called Regional Advisory Councils, and their addresses are in the *Education Committees Year Book* (see ADVICE).

Further information: Tyrrell Burgess, *A guide to English schools* (see ADVICE) ch. 9. Adrian Bristow, *Inside the Colleges of Further Education*, HMSO, 1970. Peter March and Michael Smith, *16-plus choice*, Careers Research and Advisory Centre (see ADVICE), 1972, section three: 'Going to College'. CRAC/Confederation of British Industry, *Education and Training Opportunities*. A yearbook in three volumes showing training opportunities given by various employers. The Department of Education and Science Further Education Information Service, Room 26, Elizabeth House, 39 York Road, London SE1, publishes (free) a number of booklets and pamphlets. Its *On Course Bulletins* have details of specific subjects. It also publishes *Starting Point*, describing what the colleges can offer the less academic school-leaver (ten regional editions).

Common Entrance

Entrance exam to public schools. Much emphasis on academic rote-learning, though some good attempts now being made to get away from this. Usually taken at thirteen. The papers are set centrally, but each school marks its own papers and decides its own pass mark, and they're chary of advertising their standards. Details from the Common Entrance Board, 138 Kensington Church Street, London W8.

Girls' public schools have a different exam from boys'. Taken at eleven, twelve or thirteen. Details from the Common Entrance Examination for Girls Ltd, 2 Bankfield, Kendal, Westmorland.

See also PREPARATORY SCHOOLS.

Community Schools

People who talk about community schools may mean more than one thing. They may mean the kind of school where pupils are doing social or welfare work in school-time, visiting old people, digging their gardens, or helping in playgroups or in hospitals. Or the social studies or English staff may regularly send pupils out to do surveys, interviewing people and perhaps taping the interviews.

Or they may be talking about a completely different kind of community school: one that can be used by the whole local community. Adults, and young people who have already left school, come in the evenings mainly to use the gym, the library, the hall, the workshops and lecture rooms. There may well be a special room, or a whole wing exclusively for adults, which includes a bar and a reading room.

An extension of this second type is where the users (including, perhaps, the school-children themselves) are able to play a part in running the activities of the place, whether as governors or members of users' committees.

The first kind of community school, one that uses the community as a way for pupils to learn something, is fairly common today in secondary schools.

The second kind was pioneered in the 1930s in the Cambridgeshire Village Colleges. All secondary schools in Cambridgeshire are now village colleges. Other local authorities have gradually introduced versions of the idea; they may be called community schools, community colleges, neighbourhood schools. They can be found in towns as well as in the country.

A school which is often visited by adults and where adults feel at home, is a better place for children to learn in, and a better place for teachers to teach in, than the old insulated school.

Further information: Cyril Poster, *The School and the Community*, Macmillan, 1971. Harry Rée, *Educator Extraordinary*, Longmans, 1973. The life of Henry Morris who invented the village colleges. Explains all his ideas. A. N. Sharrock (ed.), *Home and School*, National Foundation for Educational Research, 2, Jennings Buildings, Thames Avenue, Windsor, Berks., 1971, has a useful booklist.

Complaints

At the present time, few parents have any formal say in how their children's schools are run. Complaining is still their most powerful means of getting anything changed.

In the long run, the only solution is for parents to be far more involved in all aspects of school life. Even now it is better to try and do something helpful (suggest gently that the amount of homework set is overstraining the teachers as much as the children) rather than to rush straight up to school and complain (that you and your son are being driven mad by the endless homework).

However, a knowledge of the various ways of making a complaint is still an asset.

The best place to start is with the subject teacher concerned, or with the child's class teacher or year tutor. There is no point in going straight to the head unless you feel the matter is very serious; it will only make the teachers feely unnecessarily hostile.

It is likely, especially in primary and small secondary schools, that only very minor complaints can be dealt with on the telephone – and then only if the teacher involved can be called to the phone. It may even be frowned upon for anyone but the head to talk to parents on the phone. But you can always phone for an appointment.

You can visit without an appointment, but a teacher with thirty children to look after may not be able to talk easily. It's one thing to pop in for a friendly chat at the end of the day. But if you have a serious complaint – unless it is an immediate crisis – it would be better to tell them you're coming.

You should also remember, if relations with the school are bad, that an 'outsider' who enters a school (this includes parents) without permission could be trespassing, according to the law. So if the school wanted to turn nasty it could.

The teacher may not seem to share your point of view at the time. But don't assume that you haven't had any effect. Most teachers get upset and hurt by complaints though they try not to show it.

If you do feel that your complaint has been ignored, the next step is to see the head. If that fails, then you could consider an approach to the managers or governors. (This is, in fact, your only course if your child is at an independent school – short of complaining to the Department of Education, see below in this section.)

It is becoming increasingly common for state schools to have one or more parent–governors whose names and addresses you should be able to get from the school secretary or headmaster. There is no need to conceal the fact that you are taking your complaint further.

But 99 times out of 100 the governors will back the head. In independent and voluntary-aided state schools, governors do have the power to sack undesirable teachers, but many would not do this except in an extreme crisis. In ordinary state schools the kind of complaint they are most likely to act on would be one about the school building or playground.

Another line of approach might be to the parent–teacher association if there is one. At least a talk with the chairman might help you to decide what to do next.

But if you have a serious complaint which you feel a state school hasn't put right, then your safest bet is undoubtedly the LOCAL EDUCATION AUTHORITY. Start with the local divisional officer, if there is one, or otherwise the chief education officer (or director as he's called in some areas). See ADVICE for how to find him.

Again you should ask for a meeting. You may not be seen by the chief officer himself, but one of his deputies. But this will not weaken the effect of your complaint on the school.

You could write a letter rather than have a face-to-face meeting. But don't be too easily put off by that sinking feeling we all get when facing a head teacher. Many heads get it too when they have to see parents with complaints.

There is also an important point to remember in writing letters – and to a lesser extent about making unguarded criticisms of teachers. You could lay yourself open to a libel action. It would be a good idea to keep your conversations as private as possible, at least to begin with, and to make your criticisms, whether written or spoken, as accurate and reasonable-sounding as possible.

Another point about letter-writing: a letter to the head about your problems may well be read out at a staff meeting and discussed in detail by, say, fifty people. This may be what you want, but then it may not.

If your interview with the local authority fails to sort out the problem, then you have two further possible courses of action under the law. You could consider suing the local authority for not carrying out its legal duties, or you could appeal to the SECRETARY OF STATE.

The Secretary of State has powers to interfere in exceptional circumstances when a local authority can be proved to have acted 'unreasonably' (Section 68 of the 1944 Education Act).

The other possibility – suing the LEA yourself – is only for those who have time, stamina, money and – most important – a legal expert who is entirely on your side.

Other non-legal (not illegal!) courses of action you might consider, especially if all else has failed, are approaching your local MP (address from the Citizen's Advice Bureau) or telling the local or national papers.

There may also be some organization which has a special interest in the problem you are facing (see ADVICE).

If your complaint is about an INDEPENDENT SCHOOL and an appeal to the governing body has failed, then you can try writing to the DEPARTMENT OF EDUCATION. Each independent school has an inspector allotted to it who is bound to investigate such complaints. But they have power only to act on major general issues – if the school is not providing some basic teaching required by all children, if a teacher is clearly having a breakdown and putting the children seriously at risk. Moreover, in most cases, if they do act it will take months, if not years, to have effect.

Finally, a general rule. Don't take your complaint any higher up than you have to. What's the point?

See also PARENTS' RIGHTS.

Comprehensive Schools

These are secondary schools which take all the pupils – clever, average and slow – in a neighbourhood, just as an ordinary primary school does. In theory, they replace the grammar school/secondary modern system, and do away with the need to test the likely educational performance of children at the age of ten or eleven, which nearly everyone now agrees is much too early (see ELEVEN-PLUS).

Since comprehensives are supposed to cater for all the secondary school children in an area, they should ideally offer a very wide range of courses and levels of teaching: remedial help for the slowest and highly academic courses for the potential university candidates in the sixth forms.

It used to be thought that comprehensives need to be big to produce a sixth form of reasonable size – otherwise you get either a small range of sixth-form courses or a very wasteful use of specialist teachers taking two or three students at a time. The earliest comprehensives had up to 2,000 pupils.

This could have a soul-destroying effect unless the school was well-planned and organized. (Some big ones are in fact first-rate.) Nowadays some authorities, like Inner London, would prefer to have rather smaller comprehensives and share some sixth-form teaching between them. Other authorities have built them only for the eleven-to-sixteen age-range, pupils going on to a SIXTH-FORM COLLEGE after that.

In practice, things haven't always worked out exactly as they were intended to. Most local education authorities are slowly preparing to change over to one type of non-selective (i.e. comprehensive) system or another. But in many areas this change has been only partial.

The result is a situation where a comprehensive and a grammar or direct grant school are competing for students. The comprehensive will inevitably be 'creamed' to some extent – it will get a lower proportion than it should of the academic high-flyers.

This, in turn, will mean a smaller sixth form, a more restricted range of subjects taught, and possible difficulties in getting top-level staff. The school will also lose prestige in the eyes of parents who might have otherwise supported it.

However, there's plenty of evidence to show that comprehensive schools work very well, and give more chances to more children, so long as the system is properly set up. At home, polls show the majority of people preferring a comprehensive system.

When an LEA prepares to change over to a comprehensive system, it has to get its proposals approved by the Secretary of State for Education. (He or she makes a decision on each individual school.) At the same time, the LEA is bound to publish notices of the change; if, for one reason or another, you think that the proposals are not going to work, get together with nine other local electors and exercise your legal right to put your own case to the Secretary of State.

Your objections, and any others, will then be taken into account when the Secretary of State considers the change-over plans. If he turns them down, the LEA is powerless to go ahead with them.

If your main objection to your LEA's comprehensive scheme is that it isn't comprehensive *enough*, try to make constructive suggestions of your own. Mere flag-waving isn't enough; form a PRESSURE GROUP, get the advice of any teachers and other educationists who happen to be in it, and produce some alternative suggestions.

You have at least one central source of expert help, which is ready to give advice on what will work and what won't – the Campaign for Comprehensive Education (see ADVICE).

Further information: Robin Pedley, *The Comprehensive School*, Penguin, 1963 (revised edn, 1969). Margaret Miles, *Comprehensive Schooling*, Longmans, 1968. Tyrrell Burgess, *Inside Comprehensive Schools*, HMSO, 1970.

Confidential Records

Many parents get justifiably worried about the records or files that teachers and schools keep on their children, and what goes into them.

With large schools and large classes, teachers understandably cannot memorize all the relevant information about children's backgrounds and progress. So they write it down. And when the child changes schools, the information goes ahead of him. Similarly, every child has a medical record.

The danger of confidential files is that wrong or biased information gets into them and stays in them. The obvious safeguard is to make all files open to both children and parents – and many schools and teachers would be very willing for this to happen. If you or your child are at all worried about the type of records being kept, you should discuss it with the teacher concerned, and if you think it sensible, ask to see the file yourself. If he refuses, you must decide whether it is worth taking it further (see COMPLAINTS).

Confiscation and Fines

Confiscation is a fairly common form of punishment in some schools. Fines are rarer.

A teacher who permanently confiscated something would be on doubtful legal ground. We know of no rule of law which entitles a teacher in a state school to fine a child. In some cases both confiscation of property and the administration of fines could be interpreted as theft. You would need to get some legal advice before thinking of taking any sort of legal action. Don't start calling people thieves until you are absolutely sure of your legal position.

Corporal Punishment

Teachers get their right to punish children physically from parents. They have the same right as parents to punish 'reasonably'. The court's interpretation of what constitutes 'reasonable' physical punishment varies according to the mood of the times.

In maintained schools the teacher's right to punish is, in about three-quarters of local education authorities, also limited by local regulations, which set out who may punish, with what sort of instrument, where on the body, for what kinds of offences and so on. They vary widely, and interested parents would be well advised to ask to see them at their county hall. Some authorities – a very few – regard their regulations as confidential to themselves and their teachers. Every maintained school also has to keep a 'punishment book' and record in it all instances of physical punishment. In independent schools, there may be some internal regulations; otherwise punishment is limited only by the law on ASSAULT.

If you or your children feel strongly against corporal punishment, you should make your feelings known to the school, in writing, as early as possible. It has not yet been established through the courts whether a parent can withhold from teachers the right to punish his children physically. It could at least be argued that corporal punishment for minor indiscipline, if against the wishes of the parents, is unlawful. But obviously you are in a stronger position if there is a letter on file saying that you are not willing to delegate this right. STOPP – the Society of Teachers Opposed to Physical Punishment – has a standard form available for parents to fill in and send to schools. It has collected evidence of cases where the local authorities' regulations are broken by the use of instruments not allowed. They include the open hand, and the fist. Regular instruments are cane, strap, tawse, plimsoll or slipper.

Recently, some local authorities have decided to ban corporal punishment for some or all categories of children. Organized parent and child opposition can speed reform. Britain is almost alone in Europe in retaining the cane (or tawse or strap) as a standard form of punishment – and it is still used in the vast majority of schools.

Useful organizations: STOPP – Society of Teachers Opposed to Physical Punishment; abolitionist society of parents, teachers and others; holds meetings, produces regular newssheet and other publications, collects information and gives advice. Details from the Secretary, 12 Lawn Road, London NW3. National Council for Civil Liberties (see ADVICE).

Further information: Local authority punishment regulations: usually available at local education office. Peter Newell (ed.), *A Last resort – Corporal Punishment in Schools*, Penguin, 1972.

Correspondence Courses

These are learn-at-home courses through the post. You enrol with a correspondence college and they send you your reading lists and assignments. You get back comments on your last efforts together with the next assignment. Needs a strong will to keep up.

Correspondence Courses

There is a correspondence course for practically every qualification you care to think of, but some correspondence colleges are more scrupulous than others. The less scrupulous ones will lure you into taking a course which you can't cope with, you fall behind, and you still get a big bill for the course. Others get you through all right, but by the crudest cramming methods (see COACHING AND CRAMMING).

The least that can be done is to make sure that the college is accredited. (There's a committee of correspondence colleges which does this.) Ask for a list of accredited colleges from the Council for the Accreditation of Correspondence Colleges, 27 Marylebone Road, London NW1 5JS.

The National Extension College, 8 Shaftesbury Road, Cambridge, is a non-profit-making college outside the accreditation scheme whose advice might also be worth asking.

Counselling

If you are lucky you will find that your child's secondary school has a specially trained teacher to act as a full- or part-time counsellor. The function of this member of the staff is not to give careers guidance to the pupils or even to advise them on choice of subject. This man or woman has been specially trained to help adolescents with the many emotional problems that beset a person at this time. The counsellor will treat all discussions in the strictest confidence.

Although he will be pleased to see you at any time, and is anxious to be involved with parents, you must remember that he can do his job properly only if his first commitment is to the child.

Further information: Alick Holden, *Teachers as Counsellors*, Constable, 1969. Alick Holden, *Counselling in Secondary Schools*, Constable, 1971. Hugh Lytton and Maurice Craft (eds), *Guidance and Counselling in British Schools*, Arnold, 1969. Ken Williams, *The School Counsellor*, Methuen, 1973.

County Schools. See STATE SCHOOLS.

Cramming. See COACHING AND CRAMMING.

Curriculum. See SUBJECTS.

Day Nurseries

Day nurseries for the children of working mothers are run by the local social service department. Most towns have far too few of them to meet the people's need. It was a different matter during the war when the country was in urgent need of working women. Now the only children who can hope for a place are those whose mothers would not be able to support them without going out to work.

The nurseries are usually open from 8 a.m. to 7 p.m. and the children are given their meals in the nursery. The charge per week works out an average of £5 (1974 prices).

Day nurseries do not employ teachers. They are staffed by women holding the certificate awarded by the Nursery Nurse Examining Board. As well as her NNEB the matron may also have undergone a special training. Some of the nursery nurses are trained as 'wardens'. This means that they are equipped to give the older children some of the experiences they could gain in a good PLAYGROUP. Other nursery nurses have specialized in the care of very young babies. Children can be taken into day nurseries from the age of three months and stay there until they go to INFANT SCHOOL.

If you feel that your child might be entitled to a place in a local authority day nursery, then your best plan is to ask at your local Social Services Department or Citizens Advice Bureau. Day nurseries don't come under the education department, so it is no use going there for help in this matter. The Social Services Department will also have a list of the private day nurseries in your area; these are governed by the same regulations which cover CHILD MINDERS.

Deaf Children

Education of the deaf is compulsory from the age of five just as for other children, and is the responsibility of the local education authorities under the guidance of the Department of Education and Science.

Very deaf children can go to special schools from the age of two where they can learn to use what little hearing they have with the help of hearing aids and other equipment. Even a tiny bit of hearing helps, and the rest is done by lipreading. 'Deaf and dumb' language is discouraged: it only helps deaf children to communicate with other deaf children who know it too.

Slightly deaf children can be a problem. Officially the school medical authorities identify them but it doesn't always happen, and a deaf child can be labelled merely slow and stupid and sent to the back of the room when he ought to be in the front. As many as one in twenty schoolchildren are said to be slightly deaf. If you think your child may be deaf and the school hasn't spotted it, consult your GP.

The principal school medical officer will arrange for an assessment of any child who may be deaf. So can the health visitor and the local welfare department. See also SPECIAL SCHOOLS.

Useful organization: National Deaf Children's Society, 31 Gloucester Place, London W1H 4EA.

Degrees

The highest prizes in the whole education system. A bright sixth-former can expect pressure from his teachers to go on and take a degree, whether or not he wants to or has any idea of a career.

Don't force him (or her). A degree is still the road to the top professions, but does he want that? And there could be second chances (see below).

In any case, a year of employment straight after school could help the person to make up his mind. Some universities prefer candidates who have had this 'year between', so nothing is lost.

The minimum entry requirements to a degree course are two A-levels (plus three O-levels) in the GCE, or ORDINARY NATIONAL DIPLOMA. Some subject departments ask for high grades, or (and this is common) three A-levels. Some POLYTECHNIC departments might let people in on only one A-level.

There are several levels of degree. First degrees (of the 'honours' variety, or the simple 'pass') are just what they say. Higher degrees – masterships and doctorates – are normally awarded to first-degree holders who have completed several more years of study and a thesis.

University first degrees in arts subjects are usually called Bachelor of Arts (BA); those in science, Bachelor of Science (BSc). (Oxford, Cambridge and Scotland have different systems.)

All first degrees (unless you are studying for an OPEN UNIVERSITY award, or the external degree awarded by London University) call for a minimum of three years' full-time study.

A person who hasn't reached a university or a polytechnic still has a chance of putting BA after his name. The Open University exists mainly for people who missed out the first time round. A handful of technical colleges do their own degree work. The London University external can be studied for on a part-time basis; no more enrolments for full-time students can be accepted after 1976.

Employers are sometimes willing to give a second chance. Some big firms who run apprenticeship schemes will agree to sponsor a trainee, who has developed late, on a polytechnic or technical college degree course. The yearbook produced by the Careers Research and Advisory Centre (CRAC) and the Confederation of British Industry (see the further information section under COLLEGES OF FURTHER EDUCATION) lists training opportunities at individual firms.

Further information: A Compendium of University Entrance Requirements, published every year by Lund Humphries, the County Press, Priestman Street, Bradford. *Compendium of Degree Courses*, free from the CNAA, 3 Devonshire Street, London W1. *A Compendium of Advanced Courses in Technical Colleges*, published by the Regional Advisory Councils (see COLLEGES OF FURTHER EDUCATION). *Prospectus* of the Open University from the University at PO Box 48, Bletchley, Bucks. *University of London Regulations Relating to University Entrance*

Requirements, free from the Secretary of the University, Entrance Requirements Dept, Senate House, Malet Street, London WC1. *Degree Course Guides:* forty-two guides covering all the major degree subjects. From the Careers Research and Advisory Centre (see ADVICE).

Delinquency

This can mean serious and persistent misbehaviour. But if your child seems to be involved in some sort of trouble at school, make sure how serious it is before getting worried. Perhaps he's in trouble with his teachers because he has a mind of his own and has realized that schools can have stupid rules and stupid teachers too. He's not a delinquent, he's trying to assert his independence. Or if he's over thirteen and not taking exams he may be bored and not see any point in school.

If you're worried that there is a delinquency problem in your child's school, you should try and discuss it with the teachers and the head. They might benefit from an understanding of the parents' point of view. It might also mean you get a more accurate idea of the size of the problem than from the stories circulating among your child's mates.

Some people (such as the National Association of Schoolmasters) claim that violence, stealing and vandalism in schools are increasing. Others claim the opposite – that things have improved in the past fifty years. Various official surveys have been carried out but they don't tell us much. It's not enough to point to rising crime figures for young people. These may be due to more vigilant policing, rather than to any actual change in events.

If your child is delinquent in the sense of being in trouble with the police then the first thing you must have – and quickly – is legal advice. Remember that neither you nor he need say anything to the police at any time (beyond giving your name and address in certain motoring offences). Unless they have good reasons not to, the police should let you telephone a solicitor, through a friend if you want (see ASSAULT).

People have begun to realize that the juvenile courts – which deal with offenders under seventeen – are wrong for most delinquency, and in some areas this has led to the setting up of Juvenile Bureaux. If the child admits his offence, and he and his parents agree, he may (at the discretion of the police) be dealt with through the Bureau. A senior police officer administers a caution (a sort of formal telling-off) and that's the end of it. It does not remain on his record.

The child's school is informed, however. Incidentally, some children admit offences they never committed so as to go to the Bureau rather than pleading their innocence in a juvenile court.

On all matters concerning the police you would be well advised to seek legal advice, perhaps in the first place through a local legal advice centre.

Further information: D. J. West, *The Young Offender*, Pelican, 1967. *The NCCL Guide to Civil Liberty*, Penguin Special, 1972.

Department of Education and Science

The DES is the Government department which deals with all educational institutions as well as a ragbag of loosely educational matters such as the arts, museums and so on. Used to be the Ministry of Education, under a minister. Now under a Secretary of State. Grander title, same job, except that the universities come under it now as well.

The DES doesn't own any schools, nor does it run any. It does, however, make sure that all schools are run in accordance with the various EDUCATION ACTS.

The DES does not issue any instructions to teachers on how or what to teach (with the one exception, enshrined in the 1944 Act, relating to religious instruction). But it advises them, directly and indirectly, through Her Majesty's Inspectorate.

The DES's powers are much greater in relation to school buildings and equipment. The Secretary of State lays down cost limits – the price that should be allowed for per school place – for new building and oversees the costs of improvements or additions to existing buildings. The DES lays down building regulations for schools, and advises generally on architecture.

It also has a big say – almost the final say, really – in how much teachers are paid. And it has the ultimate control over the examination system.

Meanwhile, though there's a natural tendency to blame the Government for any shortcomings in education, the fault may not lie with the DES but with the LOCAL EDUCATION AUTHORITIES. These are not beyond cloaking their own inefficiencies by laying the blame somewhere else. See also SECRETARY OF STATE FOR EDUCATION.

De-schooling

Not to be confused with FREE-SCHOOLING, is the de-schooling movement, which also started on the other side of the Atlantic, and which so far exists mostly on paper – there are few actual examples of it in operation.

Though de-schoolers agree with free-schoolers that most schools are dangerously out-of-date, their solution is to abolish school altogether. Instead they want a great increase in self-help sources of learning such as libraries and directories of experts willing to take pupils individually.

Further information: Ivan Illich, *De-schooling Society*, Calder & Boyars, 1971, and Penguin, 1973. Everett Reimer, *School is Dead*, Penguin, 1971. Paul Goodman, *Compulsory Mis-education*, Penguin, 1971.

Detention

A teacher has power to keep a child back in school only for a reasonable time. And he has no right to keep a child in, *however* reasonable the period of time, if this is against parents' wishes. During the time of detention there should be continuous adult supervision.

Some local education authorities have regulations. Inner London, for instance, says detention shouldn't last more than half-an-hour. If a parent thinks a child is being kept in unreasonably long he could come into the school and demand the child. The school would have to hand the child over.

Such heavy tactics are hardly to be recommended. But you

could reasonably complain if your child has to cross busy streets to get home – after the crossing patrols have packed up. Certainly notice should be given to the parent in a case like this. See also COMPLAINTS.

Diplomas. See DEGREES.

Direct Grant Schools

There are more than 300 direct grant schools but when we use the term we usually mean a particular kind of grammar school. They are independent of the state system and, in exchange for a Government grant, they have to offer at least a quarter of their places free to pupils who have come from primary schools. The rest pay fees, but the fees are not excessive by independent school standards and if your income falls below a certain level you need not pay, although you are technically a feepayer.

The direct grant grammar schools, of which there are only 177 in the whole of the country, are proud of the mixed social classes they cater for. But in fact their pupils are predominantly middle-class. Nearly all are single-sex. Because famous schools like Manchester Grammar School and the North London Collegiate School are direct grant, it's generally supposed that all are brilliant academic establishments. This is not so. Some are no different from mediocre grammar schools.

Further information: The Direct Grant School. A Memorandum prepared by the Direct Grant Committee of the Headmasters' Conference, 29 Gordon Square, London WC1. Josephine Kamm, *Indicative Past*, Allen & Unwin, 1971, for an account of a group of girls' direct grant schools. *Public Schools Commission, Second Report*, HMSO, 1970.

Discipline

There is an enormous variation in the ways schools keep discipline. A really successful school won't think the subject worth discussing. Other schools may attach enormous importance to it. So, of course, do some parents.

When parents complain that a school 'lacks discipline' they may simply mean that they think it's too progressive. That is really an argument about the nature and purpose of a school.

So, if you hear that a school has 'good discipline', do not conclude that it must be a good school. It may just be a cruel one.

There are schools in which running in corridors, talking in class, coming to school without a ruler, or failing to call a teacher 'sir', would be regarded as breaches of discipline, to be punished. Such little things are good clues to what kind of school you're dealing with.

Punishments, again, vary a great deal. They range from EXPULSION and suspension, through CORPORAL PUNISHMENT (even, in certain schools, for such trivial things as those listed above!) to CONFISCATION, DETENTION, extra work, writing lines, and the taking away of privileges or treats such as school visits.

Obviously, the more often such things are used, the less successful a school is in 'keeping discipline'. See also RULES.

Further information: Barry Turner (ed.), *Discipline in Schools*, Ward Lock Educational, 1973.

Discovery Methods

Sometimes one hears parents complaining that children seem to do nothing but play in school these days. It is rare now to hear children chanting their tables or learning long lists of words for spelling. More and more teachers are abandoning formal instruction for methods in which the children are encouraged to discover for themselves how the world works, and in doing so learn the basic skills, such as reading, writing and mathematics which can help them to understand it.

You may hear your child refer to 'topics', 'themes' or 'project work'. This is because discovery methods usually involve small groups of children working together on some aspect of a particular subject or topic. It can be anything from Tea to the River Thames. Usually the subject is initially chosen by the teacher, who will gather together as much material (books, wall pictures, filmstrips, cassettes or records) relating to it as she can. The children will also make a collection of their own, and the project will usually end with a classroom display of the work they have done during the course of it.

This way of learning is often carried over into the first two years of secondary school; and there are several schemes, particularly in maths and science, for extending it to examination work. The basic principle is always the same: the emphasis is on learning by doing, and not by amassing a pile of information imparted by the teacher.

Further information: R. F. Dearden, 'What is discovery learning?' in *Education 3–13*, Collins, April 1973. Annabelle Dixon, 'Talking of discovery', in *Education 3–13*, Collins, April 1973.

Drama

Don't be too disappointed if your son is not chosen to play the part of Julius Caesar in the school play, or if you do not have to make angel wings for his little sister at Christmas. The rehearsed event which a school puts on for parents at the end of term can be a very good occasion but it is not the real purpose of drama in either secondary or primary schools.

From a very early age children can learn by improvised drama in the classroom. At first this activity is used to encourage children to express themselves fluently and clearly in speech and movement. When they are older it can be used to help them learn a new language or to understand an event in history. It is nothing to do with professional training for the stage.

If you think your child has special acting ability he can be auditioned for a stage school. The age for entry varies from school to school, but the general rule is eleven, which is also the normal age of transfer from primary to secondary schooling. These schools are privately run, although local education authorities will pay the fees of children who are selected to attend them.

Dress. See PERSONAL APPEARANCE.

Drugs

Here we're talking about the narcotic drugs – cannabis, LSD, heroin, amphetamines – not whisky, coffee or cigarettes to which some of us are addicted.

It's important for adults not to be immediately agitated by the very mention of drugs, and important not to be too much on the look-out for drug-taking. First, it's very difficult to spot. Second, repeated warnings against it could have just the opposite effect from what you intended: 'Forbidden fruit tastes best'.

But what should you do if it looks as though your child is taking narcotic drugs? First, keep cool. Second, go along to your doctor (if he is sympathetic) and take him or her into your confidence. A doctor, or the local hospital, would let you know about the nearest drug clinic, where specialist help and advice are available.

Your child's school could be the worst place to go – but it could be the best: a trusted teacher can be the most helpful adult of all. Some independent boarding schools automatically expel. Others are more compassionate. Some heads might insist on reporting the case at once to police and governors. Others are more cautious.

If you think your child is associating with a group whom you suspect to be involved in drug-taking, there's little you can do except suggest he look for other friends. You could mention the situation to the school, but surely one of the most difficult requests any school has to deal with is when a parent comes along and says: 'Will you please detach my child from this set he's going around with?'

Is cannabis itself physically harmful? It doesn't seem to be (and at least it doesn't cause lung cancer).

It is still against the law to be 'in possession' of narcotic drugs. But you don't get prosecuted now if your house is being used without your knowledge for 'pot' smoking parties. If you do know, however, or if you deliberately avoid knowing, you may well be vulnerable.

Further information: The best reading on the subject is in the pamphlet published by ACE (see ADVICE), '*Where on Drugs. A parent's handbook*'.
Useful organizations: Release, 1 Elgin Avenue, London W9. The Association for the Prevention of Addiction and Association of Parents of Addicts, 16 King Street, London EC2. Institute for the Study of Drug Dependence, Chandos House, 2 Queen Anne Street, London W1M OBR.

Duke of Edinburgh's Award Scheme

In Prince Philip's own words, the scheme is designed 'as an introduction to leisure-time activities, a challenge to the individual to personal achievement, and as a guide to those people and organizations who are concerned about the development of our future citizens'.

One of the scheme's brochures puts it a different way: 'Would you like to make friends, help the less fortunate, enjoy yourselves, have action?' it asks teenagers. And, in fact, the activities that go to make up the qualifications for the three awards (bronze, silver, and gold, according to the age of the applicant) cover an enormously wide range of interests.

The bottom age limit is fourteen; the top, twenty-one. Physical handicap is no bar to success.

Further information: For more details, get in touch with your LEA, the nearest regional office of the Award Scheme, or its London headquarters. The address of this is: 2 Old Queen Street, London SW1H 9HR.

Dyslexia

True dyslexia is a purely physical disability which interferes with even the most intelligent child's ability to master the skills of reading. A child (or adult) suffering in this way has difficulty in concentrating his attention on a sequence of letters and so will not naturally continually read words from left to right, with the result that they come out backwards. He keeps looking at familiar words as though he were seeing them for the first time.

Because there are so many degrees of dyslexia, varying from the extreme which no one can fail to recognize, to a slight visual confusion, some people treat a dyslexic child as a normal slow reader. If you have reason to believe that your child is dyslexic, and if you are dissatisfied with the diagnosis of either his teacher or the family doctor, write to the Dyslexia Institute or to the British Dyslexia Association. The people there will be able to tell you of specialists in this disorder working in your area.

Naturally the very best teacher for a dyslexic child is a teacher who suffers from the same handicap but who has managed to overcome it. Some remedial reading centres are lucky enough to be able to employ such people. Remember that a teacher can't hope to cure dyslexia; she can only help children to master the skills of reading and writing despite it.

It is very important that parents and teachers work very closely together in helping a dyslexic child to read. He needs practice at home, but it must be practice according to the methods adopted by the teacher, if he is not to get disastrously confused. It is also important that teachers and parents alike fully understand that a dyslexic child is not suffering from BACKWARDNESS.

Further information: S. Naidoo, *Specific Dyslexia*, Pitman, 1972. P. Meredith, *Dyslexia and the Individual*, Hamish Hamilton, 1972. Macdonald Crutchley, *Developmental Dyslexia*, Whitefriars Press, 1964 (2nd edn 1970, re-titled *The dyslexic Child*). ACE (see ADVICE) has a list of schools.

Useful organizations: The Dyslexia Institute, c/o North Surrey Dyslexic Society, Cambridge Cottage, Broadway, Laleham, Staines TW18 15B. British Dyslexia Association, 126 Buckingham Palace Road, London SW1.

Education Acts

The education system in England and Wales is governed mainly by the Education Act of 1944. This divided school education into two levels, primary and secondary, and laid down that there should be secondary education for all. Contrary to what many people believe, it did *not* define what form secondary education should take -- that is, whether it should be in secondary modern, grammar or comprehensive schools. It merely said that there should be provision for school-age children according to their 'age, ability and aptitude.'

The Act is mainly about duties – of LOCAL EDUCATION AUTHORITIES, Government, parents. It says little about their rights.

Local education authorities are charged with providing enough schools of the right kind for all the children of school age in their areas. They must ensure that the buildings are up to standard and that schools are governed properly, make arrangements for special education where it is needed, and so on. The Act makes it quite clear that local education authorities are responsible for the administration of schools – a useful thing to remember if there is any complaint about the running of a school.

Parents are responsible, according to the Act, for providing for their children's education 'either by regular attendance at school or otherwise'. What goes on in schools themselves gets surprisingly little attention in the Act.

It's useful to be able to quote the Education Act of 1944 in any dispute – but only if you know it thoroughly. The 1944 Act has been amended in a number of details and it is important to see these, too, if they touch upon the point at issue. The main amending Acts, apart from those relating to teachers' pay, are: 1959 (grants to voluntary schools); 1962 (school-leaving dates and student grants); 1964 (the age of transfer from primary to secondary school); 1967 (grants to voluntary schools); 1968 (governing bodies of maintained colleges); 1971 (local authorities empowered to sell school milk to children over seven).

Because something is in an Education Act it doesn't mean it has to happen. Provision for the raising of the school-leaving age was made in the 1944 Act but didn't happen till 1972. The

Act empowers people to do things they don't have to do: provide certain local GRANTS, for instance. It's not an awful lot of use as a parents' charter. But see PARENTS' RIGHTS.

Further information: The Education Act 1944, HMSO. William Alexander, *Education in England* (2nd edn), Ginn, 1970.

Educational Priority Areas (EPAs)

This was a phrase coined in the Plowden Report on primary schools (1967) which defined certain areas in need of extra funds because of poor housing and deprived children. Pilot experiments in four areas, completed in 1972, suggested that one of the greatest needs in such areas was a closer co-operation between parents and schools.

Further information: Children and their Primary Schools (Plowden Report), HMSO, 1967.

Educational Psychologists

As there are not many educational psychologists, they tend to have a somewhat mysterious reputation with parents and teachers since their visits are often swift and fleeting. This is nearly always because the educational psychologist is overworked, carrying a vast case-load that makes it very difficult for him to give individual children all the help they need.

An educational psychologist must have a degree in psychology as well as teaching experience and further training in this field. He is qualified in diagnosing learning and behavioural difficulties in the classroom; he should also be helpful in suggesting various remedies, where these are at all feasible, both in the school and in the home. Many educational psychologists work from Child Guidance Clinics, where they can call on the help of a psychiatrist or social worker if needed.

If the school wishes the educational psychologist to see a child over some difficulty, ideally this should come after full consultation with the parents. A school is probably within its rights, though, to consult an educational psychologist about a child without first seeing the parents, although obviously this should be avoided wherever possible. At the other extreme, if you should want your child to see the educational psychologist and the school does not agree, there is nothing to stop you contacting the psychologist yourself. You can find his address from your local education office, possibly the phone book, too, or else from the *Directory of Child Guidance and School Psychological Services*, published by the National Association for Mental Health, 39 Queen Anne Street, London W1M 0A5.

Further information: Psychologists in Education Services, HMSO, 1968.

Educationally Subnormal (*ESN*)

If a child has very great difficulty in keeping up with his classmates, is unable to read or write, or does not start to acquire these skills until a very late age, his parents may be advised to send him to a SPECIAL SCHOOL. This advice will come from an EDUCATIONAL PSYCHOLOGIST who has been consulted by the child's teachers. The decision to remove a child from a normal school is arrived at as a result of a series of tests. They aim to measure his intellectual capacity and to show whether he can benefit from conventional teaching.

Whether a slow-learning child will eventually end up in a special school for the educationally subnormal depends very much on the area his parents live in, and how many special schools the local authority has set up. In some areas it is quite usual for slow learning children who are technically classified as ESN to be taught in special classes of the normal secondary schools.

A slow-learning child in a good special school with competent, original and sympathetic teachers stands a much better chance than one left to cope in a normal school. This is particularly true if the Youth Employment Service in his area does that much extra and is sympathetic and aware when it comes to his needing a job.

Every child of school age is entitled to help from a qualified teacher, even if the child is so subnormal that he has to spend his childhood in hospital. It is the responsibility of every local educational authority to arrange this. If your child is in a subnormality hospital, and if you feel that this part of his care is being neglected, get in touch with the adviser for special education at your local education office.

Further information: C. Petrie, *Backward and maladjusted children in secondary schools*, Ward Lock, 1972.
Useful organizations: National Society for Mentally Handicapped Children, Pembridge Hall, 17 Pembridge Square, London W2.

Eleven-plus

This exam decides what sort of secondary school your child is to go to – 'selective' (grammar school) or 'non-selective' (comprehensive or 'county secondary' school). Comprehensive schools are supposed to do away with the eleven-plus, but although there are more and more comprehensive schools probably as many as half the primary school pupils in England and Wales still sit for the exam. The reason for this is that even in areas where there are comprehensive schools there are some selective schools too.

Before 1944 people called the exam 'The Scholarship'. 'Eleven-plus' is not the right name for it really, since a lot of children have to take it at ten. (Entry to secondary school is normally in the September after the eleventh birthday, but the exam is taken two terms before.)

Each local education authority makes its own arrangements for the eleven-plus. Some combine the results of an INTELLIGENCE TEST with head teachers' judgments. Others have abolished the exam itself, but have brought in another procedure sometimes called 'guided parental choice'. Parents are advised by teachers, using information they have from day-to-day school work, as to whether a child should try one form of secondary education or another.

Those LEAs which keep the exam in its conventional form make use of intelligence tests as an important part of their procedure, the idea being that it measures what a child *can* do rather than what he *has* done.

It was probably arguments based on the harm the test was doing to children and to teaching in primary schools that swung people in favour of comprehensive schools. Arguments against the eleven plus include: (1) It's inaccurate; (2) it's unfair. Whether a child passes it depends on how many selective places there are in the area, and this varies hugely; (3) primary schools are tempted to cram for it. Some once put 'intelligence' on the timetable and made children work through tests every afternoon; (4) primary schools put their likely eleven-plus successes in the top streams from the age of eight or nine – much too early for such a decision, but a great help for the A-streamers.

Can you appeal against the decision? Yes – to the chief education officer. But in most areas there are second chances, after the child has been in the secondary school for a year, often without an exam. The transfer may be recommended if the head and teachers feel that a mistake may have been made.

The important thing is not to worry excessively as this does the child no good. See also COACHING AND CRAMMING.

Further information: Procedures for the Allocation of Pupils in Secondary Education, National Foundation for Educational Research (NFER), 2 Jennings Buildings, Thames Avenue, Windsor, Berks., 1963. *Local Authority Practices in the Allocation of Pupils to Secondary Schools*, NFER, 1964. The Campaign for Comprehensive Education (see ADVICE) has up-to-date information on how soon you're likely to get rid of the eleven-plus in your area.

Encyclopedias

There is a confusing array of children's encyclopedias on the market ranging from expensive multi-volume affairs bound in tooled leather to the kind which come out like periodicals, doing, say, half a letter a month. Just watch out you don't get stung, that's all. Don't be led astray by pretty pictures accompanying an uninformed or out-of-date text. And beware of door-to-door salesmen with pens ready for you to sign on the dotted line, even if they do claim to represent the local education authority. (A not too likely story.) Doorstep buying could be dearer in the long run anyway than buying in a shop.

Equipment

Independent schools are a law unto themselves when they decide how much equipment should be provided by parents. For advice, see EXTRAS. In state schools, the theory is that all educational materials, including books, craft materials and sports equipment (but not games clothes) are free. You yourself would be expected to provide football boots, plimsolls for PE, shorts and singlet for PE or football, but the school should produce the hockey-sticks, cricket bats, and school colours for team games.

Since practice varies from school to school it's as well to find out these things beforehand. Some schools have the parents along to explain such matters. If you think you can't afford the extras, write immediately in confidence to the head teacher or have a private word with him. He may work for a generous authority. Again, the theory is that no one should be prevented from taking part in school activities merely through lack of means.

The theory has one incidental snag. Since the craft materials used are the property of the school, the nice things the pupils make from them are the property of the school too. Once again, you'll find attitudes vary here.

You may, too, find yourself having to pay up to £20 a year for materials needed for domestic science – mostly food. The idea here is that you get the benefit because the pupils bring home the finished product to eat.

A word of praise should be put in here for teachers in under-equipped schools who provide all sorts of teaching materials themselves.

See also SCHOOL FUNDS.

Evening Classes

Almost every imaginable subject, from shorthand to sea navigation, is taught in evening classes somewhere or other in Britain. Classes cater both for further education – you can take O- or A-level courses at some of them – and for such leisure pursuits as crafts, amateur dramatics, folk-dancing, and so on. They're not free, but fees are very modest, and evening classes must rank as one of the cheapest forms of leisure activity.

Classes normally run from the early autumn through to about Easter, but some – in outdoor pursuits, for example – continue throughout the summer. They are held in local evening institutes – sometimes a college of further education, but often a local school.

You can find out what's happening in your area by contacting the local education office, but for many people an inquiry at the public library might be easier.

If you'd like to have a course that isn't on offer locally, get in touch with the evening institute direct, because it's possible that other people may have made a similar request. The minimum number for a course is twelve, so the more friends you can take along with you, the better. If you want to study an out-of-the-ordinary subject (say, making corn-dollies) it helps if you know the name of a likely tutor.

Another possibility is to get in touch with the local branch of the Workers' Educational Association, which also runs evening classes, or with the extra-mural department of the nearest university. Your library should be able to help with addresses.

Further information: Adult Education, Councils and Education Press Digest (see ADVICE).

Examinations

Examinations are used either to test a pupil's achievements up to date, or to qualify him for a further step in his education or career. But they have a third function: to provide 'motivation'. If a pupil doesn't have a goal, it is argued, then he won't do any work. There are those who believe that this is the wrong sort of motivation and that if the schools taught properly children would want to work anyway – the motivation would come from within, instead of being imposed from outside.

Most teachers, however, do not take this view. For we must remember that there is yet another function which examinations fulfil: they offer a splendid ready-made syllabus to a teacher who might otherwise not be quite sure what he ought to be teaching.

Not all examinations fulfil all these four functions, but most do. 'Internal' exams set and marked by class teachers at end of term are mainly for the first (record of progress); the old ELEVEN-PLUS is entirely for the second (qualification). The GENERAL CERTIFICATE OF EDUCATION (GCE) fulfils all four functions, despite warnings from the experts that no examination can efficiently look forward and backward at the same time. This, however, is what the GCE tries to do. Its Advanced level is used as a sort of leaving certificate for employers *and* as a means to help university and college selectors to guess performance in a course of higher education.

'Multiple-choice' exams (the tick-the-right-answer kind, as found in INTELLIGENCE TESTS) are highly reliable because the marks don't depend on the mood of the examiner. They have been criticized for not testing things like creativity and imagination, but they are not by any means to be despised and can be very searching.

'Mode 3' exams are exams set and marked by teachers in the school in which they are taken, but, unlike ordinary end-of-term exams, they give a nationally-recognized certificate. (External moderators see fair play and try to ensure some sort of reliability.) The CERTIFICATE OF SECONDARY EDUCATION can be gained in this way and, in some places, the GCE. It is up to individual schools to decide whether to use 'Mode 3'. Its results are likely to be highly valid, since you don't have the teacher and the pupils working together to beat 'them', the examiners: the teacher *is* the examiner. So there is none of the question-spotting and mark-grubbing associated with external exams.

Other efforts to make exams more valid include the open-book exam (take your reference books into the exam room), the no-time-limit exam, and the miniature thesis (you are given the subject say a fortnight ahead). The difficulty with these techniques is not so much that they might lead to lowering of standards, as some right-wing educationsists and politicians think, but rather that they take a lot of time and are hard to organize in a reliable way when the examinees run into hundreds of thousands. (The same is true of 'continuous assessment', in

Examinations

which pupils are being judged throughout their courses; many colleges of education use this, and a few universities.)

For notes on individual exams, see separate entries.

Deciding what combination of subjects to go for in any exam is absolutely vital: many young people have found themselves at a temporary dead end because they've been wrongly advised about requirements higher up the ladder (see CAREERS).

What if the pupil wants to go in for an examination and the school says he's not up to it? At one time the examination boards used to ask schools not to put in what they thought were hopeless candidates, but nowadays most schools wlll give entrants the benefit of the doubt.

If the school does refuse, it's always possible for the pupil to enter as a private candidate. The boards require their examinations to be sat for in 'convenient centres', and in this case the convenient centre would be the school, so there will be no difference except that the parent will have to pay the entrance fees, amounting to a few pounds.

The private candidate could just be at a disadvantage, not having the backing of the school. A school can draw the examining board's attention to the candidate's particular merits or difficulties and the boards take a special look at results which don't square with the school's expectations. A private candidate stands alone.

Failure in an exam does not imply stupidity or laziness, though it may do so. The examiners may be wrong, the exam may be a bad one. On the other hand, ambitious parents who encourage their children to sit examinations they're not up to are doing their children the greatest disservice.

See also COACHING AND CRAMMING; DEGREES.

Further information: You can buy back numbers of exam papers from the GCE boards. Their addresses are listed in the *Education Committees Year Book*, Councils and Education Press (see ADVICE), to be found in any good reference library. CSE boards are also listed.

A quick account of the problems of trying to make examinations reliable and valid is Noel Cowen, 'Changing examinations', in *Trends in Education*, no. 6, HMSO, April 1967. It is still up-to-date. See also F. H. Pedley, *A Parents' Guide to Examinations*, Pergamon, 1964. There are quite a few books and pamphlets on the techniques of studying for exams. For example: C. A. Mace, *The Psychology of Study*, Penguin, 1969. Clifford Allen, *Passing School Examinations, A Book for Parents*, Macmillan, 1964.

Exchanges. See HOLIDAYS, SCHOOL JOURNEYS.

Expulsion

Expulsion means being sacked from school for good. It happens when a school just can't cope with the pupil any more, and it's a sort of confession of failure on the part of the school. Usual reasons: the pupil is out of control, or, more commonly, he's said to be corrupting the other pupils in some way. Some heads (particularly of independent schools) sack automatically if a boy or girl is found with drugs, for example, which can be shown to be dangerous to the well-being of the school.

In state schools a head can't expel. The governors have to do it. But a head can suspend the pupil instead, though again he'd have to get the governors or managers to confirm the suspension. Suspension means the pupil isn't allowed into school, though he hasn't been sacked.

Suspension can be just a 'holding operation' by the head till he can get the governors to agree to get rid of the child altogether. Or it can be for something fairly trivial.

There are schools where children are suspended on the spot if they arrive more than an hour late. And there are others where it's reserved for something 'serious', like stealing.

The variations are tremendous. One head will expel or suspend where another would have called sympathetically for guidance from the EDUCATIONAL PSYCHOLOGIST.

If your child is suspended, try to get all the facts straight and talk as soon as possible to the head. If you think he's been unfair, and complaining to him doesn't work, complain to the managers or governors.

Supposing he's been expelled, you will probably have the

right to appeal to the managers or governors. In any case, don't hesitate to appeal to the governors if you think the expulsion unfair. If this fails, complain to the LEA (see COMPLAINTS).

In practice it quite often happens that although the LEA has a number of expelled children on its books, no school wants to take them. It also quite often happens that these children are very near school-leaving age anyway, so that a delay of only a few months in placing them is needed before it becomes unnecessary. This situation could be a godsend to the child who has become absolutely fed up with school (may be with good reason!) and only needs a legal reason not to attend any more.

If this isn't the case and you and your child are anxious for him to get back into school, then you have every right to pressurize the LEA into finding a place.

In independent schools the practice is rather different. There are three stages: (1) rustication, which is a fancy word for suspension; (2) being asked politely to take your child away on the grounds that he doesn't get anything out of the school; and (3) straight expulsion. Many heads prefer (2) because expulsion means the pupil's name is crossed out of the school records as though he's never been there. This could also be a disadvantage in job-hunting later, and is a serious thing to do to a person. Moreover, the head can't, in law, expel except for good reason.

If your child has been expelled, you can appeal to the governors, but if they support the head – as they almost certainly will – then there is nothing you can do – except try to persuade the head not to make such damaging comments about your child to other heads that no other school will take him in.

It is quite common practice for heads to consult each other about pupils transferring mid-course. You may find that the advice of one of the independent schools advisory services would be helpful here (see ADVICE).

Extras

The published fees of a private school are no guide to the size of the bill you will eventually get. Schools vary in the amount of extras they charge, so ask for a full list of them before contracting with a school to send a child there. Note which extras

60   *Extras*

will have to be paid anyway (laundry, gear for compulsory sports, textbooks), establish their likely costs (schools can be maddeningly vague over such details and may have to be bullied), and distinguish those items which, though optional, will have to be paid for if the pupil is not to feel left out of the life of the school, and those which are genuinely extra (polo, golf?). It's worth the sweat, since the total could add as much as £200 to the yearly bill (1974 prices). Then add another (say) £50 for unforeseen extras. Some schools, for example, charge for extra tuition in weak subjects. Not all are so devious. Eton is good about not charging extras. But perhaps you weren't thinking of Eton anyway.

State schools are, of course, supposed to be free. But (unless your income is very low and you can claim a grant) UNIFORMS are not. They, and games clothes, are the biggest extra items for state school parents. Luckily, fewer schools nowadays are demanding complicated uniforms which have to be bought from a named supplier. Uniforms are more often of the sort that can be worn at week-ends without embarrassment.

A typical initial outlay for a twelve-year-old girl in a comprehensive school might amount to about £12, including skirt, gym skirt, two blouses, two white cellular blouses, two summer dresses and a leotard for gym, but not including gym shoes, hockey shoes or blazer. Outlay for a primary school child might be as little as £3 (1974 prices).

Uniforms aren't compulsory, technically speaking (there are no regulations on the point) but heads often behave as though they were, and can make the wearing of them a school rule. For an explanation of this contradictory situation, see RULES.

Of the non-compulsory extras which you may well want to pay out, the only major one is for SCHOOL JOURNEYS abroad. You might have to reckon on this setting you back, say, £80 a couple of times in a child's school career.

Another non-compulsory extra to be budgeted for is, of course, school dinners (60p a week in 1974). Again, there is a free school meals scheme for poor parents willing to undergo a means test (see MILK AND MEALS).

See also EQUIPMENT.

Family Grouping

This term refers almost exclusively to INFANT and NURSERY SCHOOLS, and means simply that children of all ages are mixed together, instead of being divided into classes according to the year of their birth. Another term for this method is 'vertical grouping'. It has the advantage that brothers and sisters can be kept together while they are young if the teachers and the parents think it is a good thing.

The chief benefit in the infant school is that it does away with the 'reception' classes. If the children are divided up into classes according to their age, then all the five-year-olds who are starting school will be put into the same class. This can often be a distressing experience for the children, all of whom are bound to feel insecure and homesick as they start school, and a frustration to the teacher, who cannot possibly do her best work if she has to try to cope with twenty-five or more unhappy children.

In a school which goes in for 'family grouping' the new children will immediately join an established class of older children; and the teacher will only have to concentrate on settling a manageable handful in at a time. On the other hand some teachers will argue that this benefit is outweighed by the fact that the six-year-olds are held back if they have to work with five-year-olds.

Further information: Lorna Ridgeway and Irene Lawton, *Family Grouping in the Primary School*, Ward Lock, 1965.

Fees

State schools charge no fees. Universities and other higher education establishments charge fees for tuition, but these are automatically covered if your child gets a GRANT. If he doesn't get a grant, you'll have to pay the tuition fees in addition to the cost of his keep. But the fees are heavily subsidized by the state and range from about £60 to £150 a year, which is nothing like the real cost.

Colleges of education will charge full costs to students who don't get a grant. The full charge for board, lodging and tuition is about £1,000 a year.

COLLEGES OF FURTHER EDUCATION charge no fees to students under eighteen. Students over eighteen pay according to the kind of course they're on, again presuming they're not on a grant.

After the age of eighteen (or nineteen if the course is of a kind which could be taken at school, such as a GCE course) the fees at an FE college would be about £50 a year.

INDEPENDENT SCHOOL fees vary a lot but a top public school could charge not much less than £1,000 a year, plus EXTRAS. But if you borrow money on a life insurance policy (the earlier the better) you can cut the cost by up to 50 per cent, in terms of earned income. So a public school career for your son could cost you only £2,000 for the four years. (All 1974 prices.).

Any insurance broker will be only too glad to tell you how it's done. The secret is the tax concessions you get on life insurance. Tax concessions also apply to gifts to your son made under covenant. If you don't know an insurance broker, your friendly bank manager will advise.

Free Schools

Free schools, here and in the USA and elsewhere, have recently been set up by people who feel that ordinary schools are so large, out-of-date and riddled with rules that they stop children thinking for themselves. For free-schoolers, learning is thinking for yourself. While a child may need a teacher's help, the free-schoolers argue that the forcing that goes on in most schools will merely put him off.

Instead of trying to feed the same information to every child, they think schools ought to be tapping the potential of each individual pupil. Under the present system, they believe this potential is vastly underrated.

The free-school movement began in the United States about ten years ago. There are now about a dozen in Britain, and many more are planned. Though each one is different, most have two things in common. They are all free in the money sense – they don't charge fees; and second, they all believe that children can only learn if they are free to follow their own interests.

Free schools are small. In Britain, none has more than 100 pupils. All have far fewer children per adult than ordinary schools. They don't think it important to have expensive buildings. Most free schools in Britain have the same legal status as independent schools. Instead of charging fees they rely on money from charities or, in a few cases, from local authorities.

Many free schools are in 'deprived' areas of large cities, because their founders feel that ordinary schools are even worse for children in these areas than elsewhere.

Further information: Jonathon Kozol, *Free School*, Bantam Books, 1972. George Dennison, *The Lives of Children*, Penguin, 1972. A. S. Neill, *Summerhill*, Penguin, 1970. John Holt, *Freedom and Beyond*, Penguin, 1973. Alison Truefitt, *How to Set up a Free School*, mail only from 57 White Lion Street, London N1.
Useful organization: Children's Rights Workshop, 73 Balfour Street, London SE17, has a list of all free schools and similar projects in this country, and sources of advice on the subject.

Games

There must be few schools where games don't appear each week on the timetable. In the primary school it may mean anything from rounders and 'tig' to attempts at cricket or soccer, usually not taken too seriously. In the secondary school, the games period or the games afternoon used always, until recently, to be filled by pupils performing or attempting some organized traditional team game. This applied to girls as well as to boys, and no one was allowed to get out of it except on medical grounds.

Today things have changed. There's now a huge variety of choices for teenagers at school, from golf and sailing to pony riding and canoeing. Athletics can now be practised for months by individual competitors. Often now the idea of forcing young men and women to be physically active for a set period once a week as a compulsory school activity has been recognized as unreasonable. In the sixth form, at least, and often in the fifth year, games are becoming optional.

There are also relaxations in many schools about the clothes to be worn for games, and about equipment to be provided by parents. As far as clothes are concerned, a school is surely reasonable to insist that children wear one set of clothes for playing a sweaty or muddy game, if they are going to come and sit in a classroom, or even walk home, immediately afterwards. If the clothes or equipment are very expensive grants may be available for parents with low incomes.

Like the prefect system, speech days and school blazers, organized games are a special feature of the traditional public schools which state schools have admiringly adopted. The public schools also encouraged the belief that games were a form of moral education, through inculcating the team spirit, grit, and so forth. This once may have been the case. But today's inter-school matches are often played with such will to win at any cost, that the moral effect may be the opposite of that first intended.

General Certificate of Education (GCE)

The certificate recognized throughout the country for getting jobs or entering college or university. The exam which grants it is at two levels: Ordinary and Advanced.

O-level is taken at about sixteen, but many schools, particularly grammar and independent schools, encourage pupils to take it earlier and get it out of the way. It has five grades, A to E.

O-level involves much learning of facts by heart and is heavily criticized by educationists – but it's still vital for entrance to higher education, and must remain so till the teachers, the universities and the Department of Education agree on a new examination system. (And about time, too.) For more on this, see UNIVERSITIES.

It's designed for the top 20 per cent of ability, but many people under this level have got through. You can get a Certificate in any single subject.

A-level is taken two years later, at about eighteen, and is also graded A to E. You need a pass in two subjects at least to qualify for a mandatory GRANT to higher education. That's the universities' minimum entrance requirement. The papers are highly specialized, some would say too specialized. Again, for the top 20 per cent of the ability range. A person doesn't have to be brilliant to get A-levels, but it's a slog. It's generally considered that each A-level subject needs eight school periods a week for two years, plus homework. Many put in more.

There's also an S- (or 'scholarship') level, not much used. It's based on the same range of study as A-level, so to pass it you don't need to know more, only to think in a more original way.

Plans for replacing the two-pass requirement with something broader, say five passes with less to learn in each subject, have been under discussion since the early nineteen-sixties.

The GCE is run by eight different examination boards. See EXAMINATIONS.

Further information: Your Choice at 14-plus, Careers Research and Advisory Centre (see ADVICE).

Gifted Children

A gifted child can either be one who has a particular ability in a subject such as music, mathematics or art; or he may be one who is a good all-rounder, being above average in both mental and physical development. About 15 per cent of the children of each age group can possibly be considered 'gifted'. Such children probably start reading earlier than most, score high on INTELLIGENCE TESTS, and are taller and fitter than other children of the same age. The usual practice in Britain is not to separate them into special classes, but to arrange for them to have access to materials which will enable them to use their powers to the full.

Fuss is made from time to time about the emotional strains and the boredom suffered by the gifted child. The answer is that he can be helped to use his gifts to overcome these difficulties. The trouble really lies in the fact that teachers expect to be cleverer than the children they teach – and this isn't the case

66 Gifted Children

with the gifted child. In order to help a child with all-round gifts, parents and teachers must use their knowledge of the world to provide him with experience that will stimulate his particular interests.

Some education authorities (exceptional, this) will pay the fees for a private establishment if your child has a special gift which the state schools can't cater for. See also MUSIC.

Further information: Dr E. Ogilvie, *Gifted Children in Primary Schools*, Macmillan Education for the Schools Council, 1973. Ann Start, *The Gifted Child*, National Foundation for Educational Research, 2 Jennings Buildings, Thames Street, Windsor.
Useful organization: The National Association for Gifted Children Ltd, 27 John Adam Street, London WC2 6HY.

Girls' Schools. See SINGLE-SEX SCHOOLS; CO-EDUCATION.

Governors and Managers

Primary schools have managers and secondary schools have governors. The rules of management or articles of government state what the powers of these bodies are.

On first reading, these may seem pretty wide, even suggesting that governors or managers control the curriculum. But on closer reading (copies can be obtained by writing to the chief education officer) it becomes clear that their powers are very limited, and that final responsibility for the running of a school lies with the head, the 'office' and the local council through its education committee. Some local authorities consider governors and managers to be so unimportant that they haven't even complied with the intention of the law; their schools are governed by a sub-committee of the education committee. Many more authorities (most, in fact) have found it impossible to give each individual school an individual set of managers or governors; one body covers a number of schools.

Sheffield and York, among a number of local authorities, have recently revised their rules and have pioneered the policy of extending the influence of governors and managers. They have insisted on the principle that every school should have its own 'body'. They have included representative parents and teachers on the boards; some have included a pupil, some the head. By advertising in the local press, they have recruited new members, unconnected with the school or the council. All major changes in the school now have to be referred to the governors or managers in advance; they are expected to ask questions, make suggestions and generally to act as linkmen between the school and the local community. With this wider and deeper involvement in the school they will not only increase their influence, but they will be better equipped to deal with the decisions which already, in almost all authorities, they are expected to take: the appointment of a new head and of senior staff; staff promotions and dismissals; the suspension of pupils.

Further information: How to be a School Manager or Governor, CASE publications, 17 Jacksons Lane, Billericay, Essex.

Grammar Schools

Grammar schools are supposed only to be for 'academic' children, which means pupils who can pass O-level of the GCE. Theoretically, this is the top 20 per cent of the range of ability. In practice the selection system (see ELEVEN-PLUS) is so inefficient that many pupils leave grammar schools with fewer than three O-levels, generally the minimum such schools expect.

Parents have no legal right to send their children to a grammar school even if they can prove, through the eleven-plus, that they are clever enough to go. The local education authority is in charge of the allocation of places and all it has to show is that it can provide a place which suits the abilities of a child – and this, of course, needn't be in a grammar school. It could equally well be in a COMPREHENSIVE SCHOOL. There are now more comprehensive schools in England and Wales than there are grammar schools.

It's silly to feel pleased about a child who has just squeezed into grammar school. He or she may only tag along miserably.

On the whole, such schools are not too good at catering for their weaker pupils, though it's only fair to say that some are improving here. The régime tends to be stricter than in non-selective schools, and the incidental expenses (games kit, uniform) higher.

Further information: Robin Davis, *The Grammar School*, Penguin, 1967.

Grants

These are paid out by local education authorities to meet financial need at almost every stage of education. The idea is that no pupil should be prevented purely through lack of money from taking advantage of the educational opportunities open to him. In fact it doesn't happen like this, because so often the size of the grant (or even whether there is a grant available at all) depends on local authorities, and some are meaner than others.

Take, for instance, maintenance grants paid to pupils who stay on at school after the minimum leaving age of sixteen. These are supposed to offset the loss of earnings that the pupil might have brought home if he had left school as soon as possible. But the allowances, which are given entirely at the discretion of the LEA, are small. Both the amounts and the income tests the LEAs give to parents applying for the grant still varied from area to area in 1974, when the new Labour Government said it would try to put this right.

Other grants for school pupils include grants for uniform, travel to and from school, school trips and school meals. The uniform grant depends on your income and on how generous the LEA is. The travel grant depends on distance from school, and the meals grant on income. Scales for these two are laid down nationally (see SCHOOL JOURNEYS; MILK AND MEALS).

It is foolish not to claim for a grant if you're eligible. Local education officials are paid to advise people on these matters, so use them!

Now for student grants. A student doing a first degree (see DEGREES), or a similar course, is eligible for a 'mandatory' grant: that is, it is his right to have one. Not all higher education courses carry the mandatory grant label, especially in the field of art education (see ART SCHOOLS) and technical education. In these cases the student will have to apply to his LEA for a 'discretionary' award.

A student's mandatory grant depends on his parents' income, and on his own if he has one. But, however rich his family is, he gets a minimum of £50 a year. The maximum grant covers payment of all approved fees, and makes a contribution to the student's maintenance.

The approved fees part of the student's grant is normally paid direct to the college or university; the maintenance is usually paid direct to the student. It arrives at the beginning of each term. Applicants for a grant must have applied to their LEA before the date on which their course begins.

Grants paid to trainee teachers at COLLEGES OF EDUCATION come under a different heading, while there's yet another set of rules governing grants for postgraduate studies.

The regulations are complicated, but the local education office is helpful. Go and see them if in difficulties.

Is it possible to live on a first degree maintenance grant? With ruthless economy, it's just about possible to manage. But most students find that vacation jobs and obliging parents are essential.

Further information: Department of Education and Science, *Grants to students 1* (first degree courses and university-based teacher training courses); *Grants to students 2* (courses at teacher training establishments); *Grants to students 3* (postgraduate study in the humanities – state bursaries); *Grants to students 4* (postgraduate study in the humanities – state studentships and major state scholarships); essential reading – especially the first. Judith Booth, *Grants for Higher Education*, Barrie & Jenkins, 1973.

Useful organization: The Citizens' Rights Office, 1 Macklin Street, Drury Lane, London WC2, will advise parents and take up cases.

Hair. See PERSONAL APPEARANCE.

Half-time Schooling

Although the compulsory school starting age is five, many schools are taking children in at the start of the school term in which their fifth birthday falls (see STARTING SCHOOL). By law a four-year-old does not have to stay at school for a full day, but it is generally taken that once a child starts infant school he is expected to fall in with the school hours. You will find, though, that you will be encouraged to take your child home for dinner during his first term at school.

If you feel that a full day at school is clearly too taxing for your five-year-old, it is usually possible to arrange for part-time attendance on medical grounds.

See also PARENTS' RIGHTS.

Handicapped Pupils. See SPECIAL SCHOOLS.

Head teacher

The wide powers given to the head teacher in Britain are the amazement of other countries (see RULES). Independent school heads are responsible only to the GOVERNORS who have appointed them (or in the case of heads who own their own schools, only to themselves). State school heads are, in effect, responsible to their chief education officers and through them to their local education committees (see LOCAL EDUCATION AUTHORITY). In practice the only thing that prevents them from doing just what they like in the running of their schools is the limit put by the local authority on their resources – numbers of teachers, equipment, buildings and so forth.

There is another limit, though. Despite their power, they are very sensitive to public opinion and they know that it is in their interests to use that power wisely. For this reason, no parent need feel intimidated by a head teacher. And there are always the governors to appeal to and, behind them, the local education authority (see COMPLAINTS).

Except in very large schools, it should always be possible to see the head by appointment. The school secretary who puts you off by saying he's too busy is doing her boss no service.

But a word of advice. Don't bluster. He's probably better at that than you are.

Further information: Brian Allen (ed.), *Headship in the 1970's*, Blackwell, 1969.

Higher Education

Higher education refers to work done by students of eighteen and over leading to a degree or its equivalent. UNIVERSITIES, POLYTECHNICS and COLLEGES OF EDUCATION are institutions of higher education. Further education, on the other hand, refers to work done at sixteen onwards not in school, for instance in a technical college.

Higher National Diploma (HND)

This is roughly equivalent to a pass degree, or just below it. Used to be the accepted 'alternative route' to professional qualifications. But the professional associations, which tend to be excessively status-conscious, have recently become somewhat less enthusiastic about it.

Higher National Certificate (HNC), the part-time version, remains a good ticket to a job as a top technician.

See COLLEGES OF FURTHER EDUCATION for more details.

HMC Schools (Public Schools)

These are the boy's public schools, Eton, Winchester, St Bees and the rest. The Head Masters' Conference, to which they all belong, limits their number to 200 schools; qualifications for belonging include a truly independent head master (though many a head master has been under the thumb of governors, usually peers, bankers, old boys and so forth); the size of the sixth form; and the number of old boys at the universities.

What are the advantages of sending a boy to a public school, assuming you can afford £1,000-plus a year for four years? In some ways, fewer than there used to be, because of that 200 limit: there are some first-rate independent schools which don't belong to the HMC.

Of the 200 only about half are what we think of as public schools in the traditional sense; that is, boy's independent boarding schools. The others are independent day schools, DIRECT GRANT SCHOOLS and a handful of state schools whose heads have been invited to join.

The advantages of a traditional public school could be listed as: small classes and good equipment, a curriculum shamelessly geared to getting pupils qualified for entry to university, and a somewhat better chance of being welcomed in certain professions which appreciate the public school type. Life at public schools is not nearly so rugged as it used to be and the best have at last realized that teenagers actually like a bit of privacy sometimes. Teaching good manners is not among the advantages. This is a myth: public schoolboys' manners can be appalling.

The disadvantages are fairly obvious. The public school world is a very special world, with its own attitudes to life. The best public school head masters are unhappy about this, and are anxious to get away from the feeling that their schools are having the effect of separating the pupils from other people. They are not always successful here.

Further information: Graham Kalton, *The Public Schools, a Factual Survey*, Longmans, 1966. Public Schools Commission, *First Report*, HMSO, 1968. *The Public and Preparatory Schools Year Book*, A. & C. Black, annually.

Holidays

Schoolchildren are not allowed to take holidays in term-time except to go with their parents on their annual two-week holiday if that comes in term.

The school holidays add up to twelve weeks a year, and the children may well find the time hanging heavy on their hands, especially in summer, and especially if all their friends have gone away and they haven't.

One home-grown solution for small children is a holiday playgroup. If they are older, they might enjoy taking part in special sports or adventure courses your local authority might be organizing in a local park or elsewhere; and in some enlightened areas, school swimming baths, playing fields and playgrounds are kept open during the summer. Some children's libraries put on special programmes, or there may even be a children's theatre.

Another solution, of course, to holiday boredom is to send your children away by themselves.

In the UK, there are holiday camps, pony-trekking holidays, adventure holidays, cycling holidays, music holidays, bird-watching holidays. Belonging to a youth club helps. Abroad, there's a wide range of exchange visits, summer schools, and young people's tours to be investigated (see also SCHOOL JOURNEYS).

When gathering information, don't forget to consult teachers at your child's school, his friends, and your friends. A personal recommendation from a consumer or his parents is worth fifty glossy brochures.

And, above all, be absolutely sure that your child is ready and willing to cope with being off on his own.

Further information: The Education Committees Year Book (latest edition), Councils and Education Press (see ADVICE). The chapter on educational travel lists a wide range of organizations catering for children and young people.

Home Education

Children who can't go to an ordinary school, say through illness, can get free home tuition through the LEA (Section 56 of the 1944 Act). The LEA decides which children qualify. Get in touch with the chief education officer.

Parents in England and Wales have the right – though few make use of it – to educate their children at home. The actual wording of the law (Section 36 of the 1944 Education Act) is that parents have the duty to educate their children 'either by fulltime attendance at school or otherwise'.

The LOCAL EDUCATION AUTHORITY is legally required to make sure that every child in its area is receiving efficient fulltime and suitable education. As usual, local education authorities differ widely in how they apply this. It seems unlikely that any authority would now go out of its way to make things difficult for a parent who acted responsibly.

In most cases, the LEA will insist that a qualified teacher is named as the children's tutor. It will also want to know what kind of timetable the child is following – though it can be very flexible. It may also want samples of the child's work, and evidence that he or she is not cut off from the company of other children unnecessarily. All this may be done by means of an interview with the parents at the LEA offices, since the authority has no right to come in and 'inspect' the home.

As the child gets older, it may become more difficult to satisfy the LEA that he has the full range of opportunities provided by a formal school. But arrangements for the child to attend evening classes, or courses at the local COLLEGE OF FURTHER EDUCATION, might get round this.

Some parents have used this legal loophole for a short period when they have been refused a place for their child at the school they wanted. In order to avoid being sued for non-ATTENDANCE, they have appointed a tutor, etc., while they kept their child out of school in the hope of forcing the LEA to provide the place they wanted.

Other parents are now wondering whether some such arrangements on a permanent basis might not suit them much better than a bad local school system. There is no legal reason why parents should not club together to educate their children at home, though a problem might arise if the arrangements began to look too much like an independent school, and subject to inspection. There are various sources of advice on educating your child at home.

The PNEU (Parents National Education Union) have a fully worked-out curriculum of postal courses for parents to teach their children. But this is mostly for families living in remote corners of the world, and the Union is stringent about taking on new families, especially ones in Britain. They will want to ask you quite a lot of questions, and charge you quite a lot of money, too. However, they say they are getting more and more inquiries from parents in this country, and are ready to help any they can.

There are not many good all-round books on teaching. Two are suggested below. For more specialized reading your main need is for a good education library which may be found in a local teachers' centre, the LEA offices or, if your LEA is part of a book-buying consortium, a centre in a next-door county.

Your nearest COLLEGE OF EDUCATION may also help here, and will very likely have an education tutor willing to discuss your plans with you, or at least give you lists of basic reading material about modern teaching methods and aids.

You could also subscribe to the Advisory Centre for Education (see ADVICE) and a magazine which gives practical teaching help such as *Child Education.*

You should also find your local children's librarian a good source of suggestions.

Further information: Child Education. Joy Baker, *Children in Chancery*, Hutchinson, 1964. Michael Deakin, *The Children on the Hill*, Deutsch, 1972. For some all-round books on teaching: John Holt, *What do I do Monday?*, Delta Books, 1970. Neil Postman and Charles Weingartner, *Teaching as a Subversive Activity*, Penguin, 1971. For further details on the legal aspects of home education: Alison Truefitt, *Alternative Education and the Law*, mail only from 57 White Lion Street, London N1.
Useful organizations: PNEU, Murray House, Vandon Street, London SW1. Children's Rights Workshop, 73 Balfour Street, London SE17, may put you in touch with other 'Section 36' parents.

Homework

Schools have no legal right to dictate how children spend their out-of-school time. So they have, in a sense, no right to insist that your child does his homework. But they do have the right to decide what courses your child may take, so they could refuse to let him stay in his present class unless he did the homework.

Unless you are opposed to the whole idea of homework (and some parents and teachers are – on the grounds that the child has done enough between nine and four and needs a rest after that) you will want to avoid such an extreme situation.

Homework problems sort themselves into two main categories: (1) There's too much of it; and (2) it's too difficult/peculiar/incomprehensible.

If either of these keeps happening, you have to decide whether the problem is traceable to a particular teacher, or whether it is more general. It would be a good idea to compare notes with some other parents.

If there seems to be one teacher who is setting what seems to be unreasonable homework, your first step should be to try and see him or her. If this fails, then see the section in COMPLAINTS. If the problem is a general one, then it is something to be discussed with your child's class teacher or the head. Children vary enormously in their capacity for individual work.

Sometimes, as exams approach, the teachers' own anxiety gets reflected in the volume of extra work they set – though a good night's sleep might produce far better results than finishing off this or that bit of work. If you feel strongly about this, the chances are that other parents do too, and a joint approach to the school could be far more effective.

There is no reason why you shouldn't help with homework, so long as you are helping your child to understand. Some teachers feel there are dangers – if, for example, you use a different lay-out for sums. But this problem can be exaggerated. The chances are that once your child understands the principle of what he is supposed to be doing, then he will also understand the different lay-outs. And you, being his parent, may be more able to spot your child's stumbling blocks than his teacher, who has thirty other children to think about.

If you are worried because you can't understand your child's homework, most teachers will be delighted to explain what they are doing.

Immigrants

How much should white parents worry if their child is sent to a school where most of the pupils are immigrants? It's a common question. A less commonly heard question, but just as important, is: how much should immigrant parents worry if their children find themselves among a large majority of white children?

Before we answer these questions, it should be pointed out straight away that no parent has any right to complain about the school his child is sent to merely because of the number of whites or immigrants in it. Put another way, you can't claim choice of a particular school on these grounds. You can only complain if your child is sent to a school which doesn't suit his aptitude or ability.

Does the presence of a large number of immigrant pupils hold back the children of white parents? Well, it can happen. But you should be very sure that it's really happening before you raise the matter with the head teacher.

You may have more cause for worry if you're an immigrant parent yourself. Official reports have shown how easily immigrant children can be held back because they have been put in classes with slow-learning white children, when their needs are quite different. What they so often need is special help in separate classes where they can catch up with their language problems.

Home-born or immigrant, you have good cause to complain if you think this help isn't being given. It's a thing which your local CASE association (see under ADVICE) might well take up with the local authority, as well as the organizations listed at the end of this entry.

Attitudes towards the education of immigrants have changed quite a bit lately. Not so long ago it was thought that the sooner they were able to mix with the rest of the population the better. Now it's begun to be realized that unless they do get special consideration (which may mean segregating them in different classes for a while longer), they are not going to be able to compete on equal terms with others according to their natural abilities.

In the same way, it used to be thought that the best way of

coping with large numbers of immigrant pupils in one area was to spread them around so that there were no more than say 30 per cent of them in any one school. Now in most areas this policy has been abandoned.

It would be wrong to grudge immigrant children the special facilities they need. Such special help, incidentally, doesn't necessarily deprive other children of facilities. A high proportion of children with language difficulties is one of the things which allow local authorities to provide extra cash and staff which they wouldn't get if the immigrants weren't there.

At the same time it might as well be admitted that the special help isn't nearly enough and that the situation can pose serious problems.

By the end of 1973 the Department of Education no longer had an official definition of an immigrant pupil. Its old definition was a child born outside the British Isles to parents whose countries of origin were abroad, or a child born to parents who had lived in the British Isles for less than ten years, but this definition was abandoned after coming under heavy fire from a Parliamentary Select Committee.

Further information: Select Committee on Race Relations and Immigration, *The Problems of Coloured School Leavers*, vol. 1, HMSO, 1969. Also from the same committee, *Education*, vol. 1, HMSO, 1973. H. E. R. Townsend, *Immigrant Pupils in England*, National Foundation for Educational Research, 2 Jennings Buildings, Thames Avenue, Windsor, Berks., 1971. H. E. R. Townsend, *Multiracial Agitation – Need and Ennervation*, Evans/Methuen, 1973.

Useful organizations: Community Relations Commission, 15–16 Bedford Street, London WC2. Publishes monthly newsletter, *Education and Community Relations*. Teachers Against Racism, 9 Huddlestone Road, London N7. National Federation of Associations for the Education of Pupils from Overseas, c/o Immigrant Liaison Officer, Town Hall, Bedford. Publishes journal, *Multi-racial School*, Oxford University Press Education Department, Oxford.

Independent Schools

Means any school which isn't a STATE SCHOOL, but is also sometimes used for an independent school which isn't an HMC SCHOOL either. There are as many as 2,600 independent schools in England and Wales alone and they come in every conceivable size and shape.

And their aims do vary. There are those which cater for parents who don't like their children mixing with the lower classes; others which guarantee exam successes through intensive coaching and cramming; others, again, which don't believe in exams but in children following their own enthusiasms. And there are the religious foundations.

Remember that the independent schools are in business to sell you their services, so they may be only too ready to give you the answers they think you want to hear. See our advice under CHOOSING A SCHOOL. Don't be too easily blinded by exam results: it may be a cramming-shop, or it may be lucky or careful in its choice of pupils. Don't assume that a marvellous staffing ratio automatically means lots of loving care: it might mean lots of repression. So if you're interested in academic standards, ask how many hours a week the pupils spend in subjects not connected with their exam work. If you're interested in freedom, ask to see the school rules. First and foremost, though, be absolutely clear what sort of school your children need. Then you can get the maximum help from the SCHOLASTIC AGENCIES, or from the Advisory Centre for Education if you belong to it.

See also ADVICE.

Infant Schools

The infant school is the first school a child has to go to by law. It can either be a separate school on its own or form part of a primary school.

Traditionally children enter the infant school as soon after their fifth birthday as possible, and stay there until the September after their seventh birthday. This means that children born in the summer will only have two years in the infant school, whereas others will have three. To get over this disadvantage, many authorities now admit children to the infant school in the term in which they become five.

If an infant school is a completely separate establishment it will have its own head teacher. If it runs as a department attached to a primary school a teacher (frequently the deputy head of the school) will be in charge of it, but responsible to the primary head teacher.

Often local education authorities have a particular official with responsibility for infant schools. The names are in the *Education Committees Year Book* (see ADVICE).

Further information: M. Brearley (ed.), *Fundamentals in the first school*, Blackwell, 1969. *Children and their Primary Schools* (Plowden Report), HMSO, 1967.

Inspectors

Head teachers and their staffs are fairly free to decide for themselves what is taught in their schools and what methods should be used. But the Department of Education and Science runs a national network of inspectors whose job is partly to keep a check on what goes on and partly to act as advisers to teachers.

Inspectors no longer carry out formal inspections designed to check the efficiency of the teaching, but they keep their ears pretty close to the ground all the same. They might well be asked to carry out inquiries following a complaint by a parent, but parents are not expected to approach them direct.

Local education authorities also maintain inspecting staffs, sometimes called advisers. Again, they are beyond the reach of the general public, though they may carry out inquiries on behalf of the local authority.

Integrated Day

Traditionally the school day is divided up into thirty- or forty-minute periods, and each one is allocated to a different subject or activity. Recently very many PRIMARY SCHOOLS have moved away from this system, which is felt to be no longer applicable when children are learning for themselves in small groups rather than being formally taught in large classes (see DISCOVERY METHODS).

The other way of doing things is the 'integrated day', and it's very common, though your child's school may not call it by that name.

Schools which have an 'integrated day' don't split it up into set times for each subject. This doesn't mean that any of the usual subjects are ignored. They arise naturally during the course of a project. For example, instead of saying, 'We're all going to do sums this morning' or, 'Now we'll do reading', the teacher may get all the children learning about, say, ships and getting together a classroom exhibition about them. This will need a lot of reading, writing, and calculation, as well as history, geography and art. And with modern methods it is quite possible for one group of children to be writing or painting while another is doing mathematics.

It's not so easy in secondary schools, where the various subjects are taught by specialist teachers. But several forward-looking secondary schools have got round this difficulty by having a group of different subject-teachers combine together to teach all the children in one year-group for one day a week, or for a whole afternoon or morning. The secondary schools call it 'team teaching'.

Further information: Mary Brown and Norman Precious, *The Integrated Day in the Primary School*, Ward Lock Educational, 1968.

Intelligence Tests

What do intelligence tests really measure? Once, it was thought that an intelligence test result – the IQ, or Intelligence Quotient – could safely predict at the age of eleven, or indeed at any other age, just what a person's potential was going to be for the rest of his life. Now we're not quite so sure.

An IQ can be quite an accurate measure of how well a pupil is doing at that moment. But it can't really tell us how he may change or develop in different circumstances, or later on.

So, while the results can still be fairly good predictors, they can sometimes be quite wrong for some people, and you can't take them as absolute, scientific measures. Nor can the results of one intelligence test be compared directly with results from a different test.

Different kinds of question in a test may often try to measure a number of different things that have been thought to be part of intelligence, such as memory, fluency with words, spatial ability and so forth. Meanwhile, no one as yet has any definite ideas as to what 'intelligence' really consists of or, in that sense, what the tests are really measuring.

Further information: H. J. Butcher, *Human Intelligence, its Nature and Assessment*, Methuen, 1968.

Jewellery. See PERSONAL APPEARANCE.

Junior Schools

Usually children stop being infants and start being juniors at the beginning of the September term after their seventh birthday.

Most junior school heads hope that the children will be able to read by the time they move from the infant to the junior school. And you will probably find that the junior school day lasts a little longer (usually a quarter-of-an-hour) than the infant day.

Most children will find the transition from infant to junior school a fairly slight matter (see INFANT SCHOOLS). In many cases it will just be a case of moving from one department to another in the same school. And the teaching methods which operated in the infant school still apply at the junior stage. Children at this age still have the same class teacher for most of the day, though they may have specialist teachers for music and physical education.

Children in junior schools are divided into classes according to age, and some schools will arrange for a class teacher to move up the school with a class, so that a child may have the same teacher from the age of seven to eleven.

It is at the junior school stage that you can most easily make your presence as a parent felt, for it is in these schools that the parent–teacher association has its largest and most active membership. And it's while a child is of junior school age that it actually likes its parents to take an interest and visit the school.

Further information: Howard Probert and Christopher Jarman, *A Junior School*, Macmillan Educational, 1971.

Leaving Age

No one may leave school till the end of the term in which he or she becomes sixteen. Those who become sixteen in the Christmas term must stay on till Easter.

The legal age of schooling is governed by the fact that there are only two possible leaving dates for sixteen-year-olds – the end of the spring term and the end of the summer term. Therefore, if a young person becomes sixteen in the five months September to January, he stays till the beginning of the Easter holiday. If he becomes sixteen in the seven months February to August he must stay till the summer holiday.

The top age for secondary schooling is nineteen.

Libraries

Nearly all secondary schools now have a library system from which children may borrow books. In many of the larger comprehensives, this library is managed by a qualified librarian. Pupils may take books home in the same way as they can from any public library.

Indeed, in most areas the public library works in very closely with the schools, and many primary schools have an arrangement whereby they borrow stock from the public libraries on a termly basis. It is up to the librarian and the head teachers whether children are allowed to take these books home. Most of them do make this possible, and speak highly of the way the books are cared for.

In primary schools nearly every classroom will build up its own library section, although making use of the central school

Libraries

library as well. In secondary schools, the central library is a much more sophisticated matter, and the book stock is naturally far larger.

Modern methods of education require that children should be capable of independent learning, and be able to look up reference books to find the information they need. In most classes in secondary schools, a period in the library will be part of the time-tabled schedule.

Further information: Janet Hill, *Children are people: the librarian in the Community*, Hamish Hamilton, 1973.
Useful organizations: The School Library Association, Premier House, 150 Southampton Row, London WC1. Educational Publishers Council, 19 Bedford Square, London WC1B 3JH.

Local Education Authorities

Although we speak loosely of the 'state system' of education, in fact schools in Britain are run not by the Government but by local education authorities – the county councils and metropolitan districts.

The importance of this for parents is that any comment or complaint about how the education system operates locally should go first to the LEA – and only if you fail to get satisfaction at this level is it worth writing to the DEPARTMENT OF EDUCATION or to your local MP. It's not a good idea to phone the education office unless you need a straight yes or no answer on a simple query; apart from anything else it'll take ages to track down the right person to speak to. If you write, address your letter to the chief education officer – and don't be surprised if the reply is delayed.

There is another way of contacting your LEA, if a letter to the chief education officer fails. Local education authorities are the education committees of the county councils (or metropolitan district councils) and local councillors have a duty to take up questions raised by ratepayers. If you don't know the name of your local councillor (and many local councillors are virtually invisible except at election time) the council offices will tell you.

Some LEAs are secretive about certain vital information, such as the names of governors or managers or even, if you can believe it, their own schools. Many will not, for example, tell you about different schools' examination records or the number of pupils primary schools send on to grammar schools. This last point may not matter – but secretiveness about simple names of schools is inexcusable and should be exposed in every way you know, including writing to the local press.

Further information: William Alexander, *Education in England* (2nd edn), Ginn, 1970. *Local Government Reorganization*, Councils and Education Press Digest, 1973 (see ADVICE). John Pratt and others, *Your Local Education*, Penguin, 1973.

Maintained Schools. See STATE SCHOOLS.

Maintenance Grants. See GRANTS.

Maladjusted Pupils. See SPECIAL SCHOOLS.

Managers. See GOVERNORS AND MANAGERS.

Maths

Modern maths plays down the importance of mere calculation and emphasizes the understanding of how maths work.

Certainly, one of the results is that children are able to cope with more sophisticated maths than they could under the old syllabus. But another incidental effect is that the ability of most parents to help with school maths at home is now strictly limited – and probably best not attempted.

An enlightened school going over to a 'modern maths' syllabus would get parents together to explain the change. But unfortunately too many fail to consider parents in this way. In this case, an interested parent could try to learn alongside his child – but this assumes that the child is being taught well. If it is evident that he is also baffled, some way should be sought of discussing the problem at school, preferably in company with the child so that he can explain his difficulties.

Modern maths teachers have a reputation among parents for neglecting 'tables'. Modern maths doesn't mean necessarily that a child doesn't know or learn his tables. Many teachers do encourage learning them but only after the child has understood what they mean.

Further information: Mathematics in Primary Schools, Schools Council Curriculum Bulletin No. 1, HMSO, 1972. *The New Mathematics*, Councils and Education Press Education Digest, 1971. *Midlands Mathematics Experiment* publications from Harrap; *Schools Mathematics Project* publications from Cambridge University Press (the *Midlands Mathematics Experiment* and the *School Mathematics Project* are schemes for secondary schools). *I do and I Understand*, W. R. Chambers (Edinburgh), and John Murray (London), 1967; introduces the Nuffield Maths Project. J. D. Williams, *Teaching Technique in Primary Maths*, National Foundation for Educational Research, 2 Jennings Buildings, Thames Avenue, Windsor, Berks., 1971.

Medical Inspections

All children are medically inspected by the school doctor at least twice in their school careers – once near the beginning and once near the end. There is often another inspection somewhere about the time of transition from primary to secondary school.

Parents have a right to be present at these inspections (and at dental inspections, which are held separately) and notice is normally given a week or two in advance when inspections are coming up. It is wise in any case to attend.

School doctors are prepared to discuss their inspections fairly freely, and to give advice if there is any need for a case to be referred to someone else, a specialist for example. But their reports, given on official forms, remain confidential to the school.

Middle Schools

Middle schools, a sort of cross between primary and secondary schools, are being developed in some areas. They come in a variety of types. They may take children from eight to twelve, nine to thirteen or ten to thirteen. Their supporters say the teaching in these 'middle years' should be turned, if anything, towards the methods and curriculum of primary schools.

But secondary school teachers have claimed that school subjects like Science and French need to be approached in a secondary style long before the age of thirteen. So the middle school itself, as well as the idea of the middle school, is bound to be something of a battle ground; some have cruelly called it the muddle school.

Those in favour of the middle schools point out that there seems to be a period somewhere between eight and thirteen when children are at a common stage of development. Most of them can read, write, add and subtract; they are beginning to think logically and are becoming less dependent on adults. They need therefore, as a group, to be treated differently.

Further information: Towards the Middle Years (DES pamphlet no. 57), HMSO, 1970. A. M. Ross and others, *Education in the Middle Years* (Schools Council Working Paper no. 42), Evans/Methuen Educational, 1972.

Milk and Meals

Your child is not entitled to free milk at school once he passes his seventh birthday, unless milk is found to be necessary for medical reasons. All school children from the age of five until the time they leave school are entitled to get dinner on the school premises.

School meals cost the same (12p a day in 1974) whatever the age of the child, and most schools ask that this payment be made weekly; the class teachers have to collect the dinner money.

A reduction is made for members of a family attending the same school, and if your income is below a certain weekly minimum, your child is entitled to free school dinners. These rates are revised from time to time; the current figures should be available from your local education office.

Free dinners are a confidential matter between you and the school, and should not be made public to the other children.

As far as possible schools will cater for children with special dietary requirements. In large schools it should always be possible to get vegetarian foods. If you want your child to stay at school over the dinner hour but not to eat the school dinner, he may bring sandwiches.

Music

In more and more schools nowadays it's possible to get free personal tuition in playing a musical instrument in school-time. Perhaps one or two fellow-pupils might be sharing the lesson. In the first instance the instrument would be provided, too, though poorer local education authorities might not be able to provide the less common instruments. If your child does well, you'll be encouraged to lay out some money on one yourself, and this could be expensive: a bassoon in good shape could set you back as much as £300. In the big secondary schools your child will be unlucky if he doesn't get a chance of some orchestral playing.

Alternatively, there are the rural and county music schools. Fees may be as low as £10 a term (1974 prices). Private teachers' fees are much larger by several times.

If exceptional talent appears, there's a scholarship offered by the Royal Academy or Royal College of Music for eleven-year-olds. Earlier, at seven or eight, very talented children can apply for entry to one of the special music schools, at Cheetham's, Manchester; at Wells; at the Purcell School, Hampstead; or at the Yehudi Menuhin School. You can get local authority grants.

For boys, there are the cathedral choir schools. They offer a few scholarships to eight-year-olds: a tough life, singing, probably learning another instrument, and getting a fairly academic education at the same time.

The eight grades organized by the Royal Schools of Music

measure an instrumentalist's progress; after Grade VIII, there's the Licentiateship of the Royal Academy of Music (LRAM), which needn't be taken at the Academy. There is a teaching and a performing version. For those who want to go to one of the music colleges, five O-levels plus an audition are the barriers. In all this, it has to be remembered, first, that thousands of promising teenagers fade out when they grow up, and second, that the competition is terrific.

Further information: **Music in Schools** (Department of Education Pamphlet no. 27), HMSO, 1969.
Useful organizations: **Rural Music Schools Association**, Little Benslow Hills, Hitchin, Herts. **Choir Schools Association**, Cathedral Choir School, Ripon, Yorks. **Schools Music Association**, 4 Newman Road, Bromley, Kent.

Nursery Schools and Classes

It is still only the fortunate few who can get their three- to five-year-olds into a nursery school or nursery class. If you are lucky enough to get such a place, it will probably be on a part-time basis, either on five afternoons or five mornings a week.

Each session usually lasts about two-and-a-half hours, and you will be expected to take your child to and from school, and be encouraged to play an active part in the life of the nursery school. Nursery education is not meant as a convenience to working mothers, but as an essential experience in a child's development. A working mother of children below the age of five must look to DAY NURSERIES or CHILD MINDERS to solve her problem.

Nursery schools are autonomous and run by a head teacher. Nursery classes are attached to an INFANT SCHOOL.

At this stage your child will not be encouraged to start to learn to read or to understand numbers. He will be able to play with sand and water in a way that is not possible at home; he will start experimenting with painting in strong colours on large sheets of paper, and he will begin to experiment with the matching of shapes and symbols. He will have opportunities to dress up and to indulge in all sorts of fantasy play from keeping house to driving buses.

Above all he will gain the confidence and independence that comes from mixing with children of his own age.

Further information: G. M. Goldsworthy, *Why Nursery Schools?*, Colin Smythe, Gerrards Cross, 1971. Joan Cass, *The Significance of Children's Play*, Batsford, 1971. Willem van der Eyken, *The Pre-school Years*, Penguin, 1967. *Nursery Education* (Department of Education Circular 2/73), HMSO, 1973.
Useful organization: Nursery Association, 89 Stamford Street, London SE1 9ND.

Open Plan

Open plan building in schools, as in homes and offices, is designed to give everyone a free access to all parts of the building, and to ensure that no part is completely cut off from the rest. The chief advantage is that it puts an end to the isolation of individual teachers, separated from other adults and isolated all day in the four walls of the classroom. The disadvantage is that it needs very careful teacher organization if the children are not to get too noisy in their activities. Some teachers dislike the system because they don't really like to be constantly in the sight of their colleagues.

Various compromises have been successfully worked out. Some schools are able to keep both systems running, giving the children and teachers who are happier working in an ordinary classroom the chance to do so, while the rest work together in the open plan areas. Another method is to have sliding dividing walls so that a room can be made whenever such a division is needed.

Only INFANT and JUNIOR SCHOOLS are ever built entirely on an open plan scheme, although some secondary schools may have an open plan area in which two or three classes can work together.

Partly, one suspects, because architects welcome the challenge of new designs, the numbers of new junior and infant schools being built on an open plan system is slightly increasing.

Open University

The University awards degrees on the basis of correspondence courses backed up by radio and television programmes. Tuition is also given at local centres and at residential summer schools lasting a fortnight. You would have to work at least twenty-eight hours a week during term-time for three years to get an ordinary degree.

There's no entrance requirement, but you will be advised whether you are likely to be able to cope with this rather tough proposition or whether you should first do some preliminary work. The National Extension College (see CORRESPONDENCE COURSES) has its 'Gateway' courses for this purpose.

The Open University is meant for adults who missed out on higher education. It does take a very limited number of eighteen-year-olds.

Fees are low. Get the prospectus from the address below.

Further information: Jeremy Tunstall, *The Open University Opens*, Routledge & Kegan Paul, 1974. Address: Open University, Walton Hall, Milton Keynes, Bucks.

Ordinary National Certificate (ONC)

The ONC is the part-time equivalent of OND, taking usually two years. The standard is as difficult but the ground to be covered is smaller. Leads to technical jobs. Minimum age of entry: sixteen. Commonly taken by employees released by their firms by the day or for longer blocks of time. Can also be taken in the evenings.

Ordinary National Diploma (OND)

The OND is a two-year, full-time course at a technical college starting at sixteen-plus and leading to a nationally-approved qualification equivalent to GCE A-level, but vocational rather than academic in content. You need four O-levels to get on an OND course. The college sets and marks the papers, with assessors from outside.

Though vocational, it's in many ways broader than many of

the A-level courses taken by science specialists. Someone doing OND in Building, for example, might find he has to take English, general studies, mathematics and environmental science as well as the obvious technology of the subject.

Universities accept OND and ONC instead of GCE, at least for some courses, though they might want a 60 or 70 per cent pass mark. POLYTECHNICS accept them for their degree courses.

Further information: For some specimen OND courses see, for example, *Schools Council Working Paper No. 45*, pp. 106–10, Evans/Methuen, 1972.

Parents' Rights

Section 76 of the 1944 Education Act says that 'the Minister (now the Secretary of State) and local education authorities shall have regard to the general principle that, so far as is compatible with the provision of efficient instruction and training and the avoidance of unreasonable public expenditure, pupils are to be educated in accordance with the wishes of their parents'. No one was entirely sure what this meant, if it in practice meant anything at all, until a test case in 1966, when a parent sued Ealing borough council for not giving parents a choice under its scheme for comprehensive schools.

The judge said he thought Section 76 must refer to such matters as the curriculum, and what kind of religious instruction was given, and whether the school was mixed or single-sex, and matters of that sort. It did not (he said) refer to the size of school or conditions of entry.

So parents don't seem to have much choice over the type of school. But the Department of Education's *Manual of Guidance: Schools No. 1* (HMSO, revised 1960) gives some useful advice. Good reasons for wanting a particular school, it says, might include: (1) convenience to get to and the avoidance of traffic dangers; (2) brother or sister at the school, who could escort younger child to and from school; (3) special facilities which other schools don't offer, such as a particular kind of advanced work which the child is good at; (4) medical reasons; (5) preference for a single-sex or mixed school. But you can't be sure about this last one being effective – for one thing, there are fewer single-sex schools than there used to be. The Muslims in Bradford have had difficulty here.

For more about choice of schools, see CHOOSING A SCHOOL. Note that the local authorities won't accept your choice if it means spending too much money – on heavy transport costs, for example.

What the Act does make clear, however, is that the parent *must*, be consulted about his child's education, once he's in school. The parent may, again, be overruled, but he must be allowed to put his point of view.

There's a nasty little section in the same Act which allows inspectors to enter schools, implying that if you're not an inspector you have no such right. In practice this means that you can't just march into the place to see how the kid is getting on. You have to have lawful business with the head or a teacher. (On the other hand, you are on reasonably good ground if you go in because the child has left something at home and you want to hand it over. Though there's no absolute right of entry, a school which put a notice saying, 'No parents beyond this point' probably wouldn't do too well if the matter actually came to court.)

But if Section 76 isn't much help to parents, there are two other sections in the Act which are. One is Section 8, which says local authorities have a duty to provide education suited to the child. The other is Section 68, which gives parents the right to appeal to the Secretary of State if they think the authority is acting unreasonably. For example, a parent whose child is suspended from school might demand alternative schooling. If he doesn't get it, he could appeal under Section 68, though admittedly he might not succeed. This applies not only to children of compulsory school age. You could put up a case for pupils even up to the age of nineteen.

The fact remains that the law is deliberately vague because it assumes that everyone, schools and parents alike, behaves 'reasonably'. The courts may decide what 'reasonably' means. To take another example; the law says that a school is *in loco parentis*. But a head teacher who made use of this authority to insist on all sorts of rules and regulations which parents didn't like, would get nowhere in court.

The school's rules don't apply only in school, by the way. The rules can't say much about the way pupils behave at home. But it's doubtful whether individual parents' objections would carry much weight if there were a rule covering, say, misbehaviour in streets around the school after school hours, and on a school bus.

The *Schools Regulations 1959* (see ATTENDANCE) make it clear that a head teacher can't refuse to take in a pupil merely because he doesn't want him. In other words, if your local junior school has empty places, your normal, healthy seven-year-old has a right to take one.

Since it's the duty of a local authority to keep the schools open for 400 sessions (a morning or an afternoon) a year, you might think you had a good case if a teachers' strike or a shortage of staff deprived your kids of part of their schooling. It's not so easy as that, though: the authority could claim it wasn't responsible for a breach of contract by its employees. You could sue the striking teachers, but no one's tried that one yet so far as we can discover! And in any case, the regulations give the school a let-out by saying they must open for 400 sessions 'apart from unavoidable cause'.

For more on parents' rights see also DETENTION, EXAMINATIONS, and RULES.

Further information: Parents and the Law, Advisory Centre for Education (see ADVICE). Manual of Guidance Schools No. 1: *Choice of Schools*; published for the Department of Education and Science by HMSO, first issued 1950, reprinted 1967. Hilary Elgin, *The Law and the Teacher*, Ward Lock Educational, 1967. G. Taylor and J. B. Saunders, *The New Law of Education* (7th edn), Butterworth, 1971.

Personal Appearance

If they want to, head teachers can make school uniform or clothing (down to the last detail – colour of socks, tights, etc.), jewellery, length of hair, etc., matters of school discipline and so within their power to control. In several cases, parents of children who have been sent home for having long hair and subsequently refused to get it cut, have been successfully prosecuted for non-attendance. But heads who object to long hair because it gets in pupils' eyes or interferes with their domestic science can always issue hairnets when necessary. Some actually do this. You could suggest this solution if a head asks your child to have a haircut.

Perhaps it is because length and style of hair have had an almost religious significance since Samson's day that many teachers seem to regard them as symbolic tests of their authority over pupils. In many schools the head teacher's discretion extends to his own staff, forbidding female members to wear trousers, and refusing to admit long-haired students on teaching practice.

You may find your eight-year-old son refused admission to his primary school because he is not wearing shorts, your daughter sent home because of that rather extravagant necklace or her giant wedgies (or whatever the current fad is). As an individual parent you have little hope of success if you decide to fight. After all, you are taking on one of the great legal power-figures of our age, the head teacher. On the other hand, if you can find enough support among other pupils and parents you are probably in a strong position.

Playgroups

Playgroups are usually run by private individuals or by committees of parents linked to the Pre-school Playgroups Association; some are organized by charities such as the Save the Children Fund. Most playgroups have a supervisor who has had some training or experience with young children, and she is assisted by a rota of mothers.

Most groups operate on two or three mornings or afternoons a week only. They very rarely take place in special buildings, but rent church or community halls. The charge for playgroup attendance can be as high as 25p a session (at 1974 prices).

The pre-school playgroup movement is largely a self-help arrangement, and although it can't offer a child all the advantages of a good nursery school it can give him the companionship and stimulation which is not always available at home.

Playgroups, as the name suggests, are centred on play, which is the most important work a child of this age can do. Properly arranged play prepares him for learning to read and the other activities he will meet in the infant school. Playgroups also prepare children for school by making them aware of a world outside their homes.

If you can't find a playgroup in your area, write to the Pre-school Playgroups Association, which will put you in touch with your nearest branch secretary. If there is no playgroup near you, then remember that they are run as voluntary organizations, and so the volunteer may have to be you.

Further information: Eileen Molony (ed.), *How to form a playgroup*, BBC Publications, 1967, revised 1970. Willem van der Eyken, *The pre-school years*, Penguin, 1967.
Useful organization: The Pre-school Playgroups Association (see ADVICE).

Politics

Teachers are as likely as anybody to have political prejudices. Should they allow them to influence their teaching? It's an argument which is likely to become more common as the school curriculum opens itself to more 'real life' influences.

Already there have been rows about MPs using school visits to spread party propaganda and to try and catch the new eighteen-year-old voters. But the risk of this sort of propaganda seems a small price to pay for an attempt to raise the abysmally low political consciousness of the population.

Teachers cannot be expected to adopt an artificial neutrality as they enter the school gates. Before you rush to complain at the 'outrage' of your child being exposed to a party-political speaker decide whether you are defending some general principle or merely exercising your own prejudices. Education should be giving children the opportunity to make responsible decisions for themselves: withholding information and pretending conflicts don't exist won't help that process.

Further information: David Rubenstein and Colin Stoneman (eds), *Education for Democracy*, Penguin Education, 1970.

Useful organization: Politics Association (association of teachers who believe that politics should be an accepted part of the school curriculum) based at the University of Sheffield, Sheffield S10 2TN.

Polytechnics

The main alternative, with the colleges of education, to the universities in terms of degree work (see DEGREES).

Polytechnics' courses tend to lean to 'applied' studies – such as management training, town planning and so forth.

They also do courses that lead to their own diplomas, to professional qualifications, and to the HIGHER NATIONAL DIPLOMAS. All courses are listed in the handbook produced by the Committee of Directors of Polytechnics (see below).

In general, applicants need a minimum of two A-levels, although the minimum requirement for HND students is one A-level only. It is often possible for a diploma student to switch to a degree course if he can convince the polytechnic authorities that he is good enough, or from degree to non-degree work, which a university student can't.

For many aspiring degree-holders this is not just an alternative to the university route, but a *better* alternative. Students there often say that the polytechnic atmosphere is less claustrophobic than that of the campus universities; that the courses are more relevant to the needs of present-day society; that the spell of work in industry often sandwiched into the courses gives an invaluable introduction to working life; and that polytechnic graduates are better placed for job-hunting.

Further information: The Committee of Directors of Polytechnics, *Handbook of polytechnic courses* (latest edn), Lund Humphries. Eric Robinson, *The New Polytechnics*, Penguin, 1968. John Pratt and T. Burgess, *Polytechnics, a Report*, Pitmans, 1973.

Preparatory Schools

Fee-paying schools for the seven-to-thirteen age-range. Their traditional purpose has been to get pupils into the public schools (hence the name 'preparatory'). At this they are extremely good.

So if you really want your child to go to public school, this is the way in. Usually, there's no entrance exam to get into prep. schools. Some are boarding, some day. The better ones nearly all belong to the Incorporated Association of Preparatory Schools. There are about 500 of these and all have been RECOGNIZED AS EFFICIENT, for what that's worth.

Most IAPS schools are still for boys only; a few are going co-educational. The girls' prep. schools usually transfer their pupils to secondary schools at eleven or twelve.

The schools are not usually particularly good at getting children through the ELEVEN-PLUS. Their work is quite different from primary schools' and far more academic, starting languages earlier, and teaching such things as history and geography as separate subjects far sooner than state schools do. This is not much fun for not-so-clever children.

Prep. schools used to have a reputation for dull teaching and for turning boys into young gentlemen, which was what most of the parents wanted anyway. It's only fair to say that the best ones are much livelier in their teaching these days, and are not so stuffy, though they do still tend to be very middle-class places. If you don't mind that, and if you can afford it, and the local primary schools are no good, it would be reasonable so far as the work goes to send a child to a prep. school till eleven and then on to a comprehensive school, or you could transfer to a grammar school at thirteen.

The best thing about them is their small classes and their undeniably happy family atmosphere. See SCHOOLS, LISTS OF.

Useful organizations: Incorporated Association of Preparatory Schools, 138 Church Street, London W8. Choir Schools Association, The Cathedral Choir School, Ripon, Yorks. Association of Headmistresses of Preparatory Schools, Meadow Brook, Abbot's Drive, Virginia Water, Surrey.

Pressure Groups

Pressure groups are what the name suggests: groups of people banding together to put pressure on the authorities to change things in one way or another. They work in two ways. First, they spread information and opinions which bring in members. Second, they help or encourage their members to make a fuss in the corridors of power – say in the local education authority – in order to advance their aims. Doors (it's hoped) are thereby opened, and sometimes action follows.

Parents of school-children are often in a hurry for change because their interest usually lasts only as long as their children are at school. This explains the large number and high activity of educational pressure groups. The most active is probably the Advisory Centre for Education (see ADVICE). The centre makes use of educational experts to spread information about a very wide area of education, and also to offer advice to individual parents who write in for it. It runs conferences for teachers and for parents, and publishes a regular monthly magazine, *Where*, as well as occasional papers of interest to parents and teachers (such as *Where* on Drugs). ACE is biased neither to state nor to independent schools, but its members are largely middle-class.

The Confederation for the Advancement of State Education is concerned only with state schools. The majority of its members are parents who send or expect to send their children to state schools and want to see the schools improve. But the membership also includes teachers, administrators and local politicians. The Confederation covers the country, and in theory every local authority area is served by a local CASE group which holds regular meetings and sends a delegate to the national conference each year. CASE publishes a news-letter every two months called *Parents and Schools*.

The National Confederation of Parent–Teacher Associations encourages existing PTAs with advice and information. Anyone wanting to set up a PTA should write for help. Its journal, *Parent–Teacher*, appears twice a year.

There are quite a number of specialist groups whose names and addresses are at the end of other entries in this book. Anyone interested should write to the secretary in each case.

Not all pressure groups are national. The CASE groups are

examples where a local community can be affected by neighbours working together. And in a single school a parents' association or a parent–teacher association can also do a great deal. There may be opposition from the school to such an association, and though on the face of it this is foolish, it's possible to see how it can happen: sometimes a small group of parents who talk a lot and put on the pressure can stop a school from doing something most parents would really want, such as arranging for sex education or abolishing expensive school uniforms. But pressure groups can be made to work more positively than this.

Primary Schools

All primary schools are divided into INFANT (five to seven) and JUNIOR (seven to eleven) sections, which may come under the same head teacher or exist separately from each other. There are no general public examinations in the primary school itself, and few primary teachers will expect children to do homework. This should mean primary school heads are free to arrange the school work in a way which will be best for the children. No two primary schools follow identical patterns, yet British primary schooling generally is internationally acclaimed as the most forward-looking in the world.

This does not mean that there are not some very poor and mediocre ones. There are, for example, still a few which gear too much of their work to the ELEVEN-PLUS selection test, where it still exists. They coach the likely children for this and neglect the others. Some have an eleven-plus STREAM: a child who isn't in that stream has been, in a way, condemned. Try to avoid that sort of school if you can: it may have good eleven-plus results, but it's doubtful if it's good even for clever children.

If you are able to choose between two or three schools, you will naturally want to meet the head teachers and see over the school. It is very important to children that their parents should take an active interest in their primary education. For this reason you will want to choose a school where the head teacher and his staff welcome visits from the parents and make themselves available to talk with them. Don't be put off by the fact that most schools run an appointment system; they have to, as a practical necessity.

Further information: Children and their Primary Schools (Plowden Report), HMSO, 1967. John Blackie, *Inside the Primary School*, HMSO, 1967. J. J. B. Dempster, *What's Happening in the Primary Schools?* David & Charles, 1973. Leonard Marsh, *Alongside the Child in the Primary School*, A. & C. Black, 1970. *British Primary Schools Today*, Macmillan, a series of booklets documenting the work of British primary schools.

Progressive Schools

Nowadays when we talk about progressive schools we tend to mean state-maintained schools which use modern methods of education. More often primary schools than secondary, they use the INTEGRATED DAY instead of an old-style timetable, they teach the new MATHS, they may have TEAM-TEACHING and be built on an OPEN PLAN; they don't STREAM their pupils, and they don't believe in the cane.

But originally a 'progressive' school meant an independent school, part of a distinct movement with certain beliefs which started towards the end of the last century and reached its height in the 1920s. Those who belonged to this movement believed that man is born good – an idea which conflicted with Christian doctrine and therefore with Christian education, which thought that original sin had to be beaten out of the little devils.

In practical terms, what distinguishes this kind of progressive school from other schools is that staff rarely compel pupils to learn. They set up, as they say, 'learning situations'. With no compulsion, when pupils do set themselves to a task, whether it be digging the garden or learning a poem, they do it with a will – of their own self-regulated will.

Many progressive schools were started in the 1920s, often by parents who wanted something less harsh for their children than was offered by the traditional public school. They were always mixed, and usually far away in the country, and always fee paying. Staff would be called by their christian names, as well as the children. Children would be free to attend lessons or not, as they wished; examinations were classed with corporal punishment as unthinkable.

Apart from the late A. S. Neill's Summerhill, almost all these ventures have succumbed to pressure from today's parents and become much more conscious of public examinations. With the public schools beginning to admit girls and generally relax their spartan traditions, there's a flow towards a middle-ground policy. The need for progressive schools seems to have diminished. However, alternative schools have now appeared (see FREE SCHOOLS) and, unlike the old progressives, they are mainly providing for the children of the poor in the heart of the city. Like the progressive schools of the past, they may well be having an influence on the normal state school – even here compulsion is less prevalent than it was, and the atmosphere more relaxed (for example, see GAMES).

Further information: A. S. Neill, *Summerhill*, Penguin, 1970. W. A. C. Stewart and W. P. McCann, *The Educational Innovators* (2 vols), Macmillan, 1967 and 1968. H. A. T. Child, *The Independent Progressive School*, Hutchinson, 1962. Ray Hemmings, *Fifty Years of Freedom*, Allen & Unwin, 1972. Maurice Ash, *Who are the Progressives Now?* Routledge & Kegan Paul, 1969.

Public Schools. See HMC SCHOOLS.

Pupil Power

The pupil power movement wants more say for pupils in the running of their own schools. Its supporters think they're not given enough responsibility and they don't like the way they are taught. They don't want to be told what to think.

In its more moderate form, the movement wants to abolish uniforms, corporal punishment and rules about personal appearance. It believes in CO-EDUCATION, more power for teachers, parents, pupils and governors and much less for the head, and a reform of the examination system. In its most radical form, it wants the schools run by committees of pupils, teachers, parents and workers, and sees itself as part of the class struggle.

The two main organizations concerned are: (1) The Schools Action Union: Organized a one-day strike in 1971. The more radical of the two; (2) The National Union of School Students: an independent offshoot of the National Union of Students.

Both these organizations have suffered from a lack of finance and a changing leadership. But there are signs that the situation is changing and that pupils are gaining more power in a system that is, after all, designed for them.

Both organizations, incidentally, dislike the label 'pupil power'. They point out that it's not just power for pupils that they want. If your son and daughter comes home fired with enthusiasm for one of these organizations, don't explode. Have a look at their aims – you may find you agree with them.

Further information: Little Red School Book, Stage I, 21 Theobalds Road, London WC1. For children's views on school, see E. Blishen (ed.), *The school that I'd like*, Penguin Educational, 1973. See also SCHOOL COUNCILS.
Useful organizations: National Union of School Students, 3 Endsleigh Street, London WC1. Schools Action Union, 75a Acre Lane, Brixton, London SW2. National Council for Civil Liberties, 186 King's Cross Road, London, WC1.

Reading

Should you teach your child to read? Most teachers will ask you not to, for they say that as methods are bound to be different you will probably only confuse him; for this reason we can't recommend any of the various teach-your-child-to-read books now on the market.

This doesn't mean that you should not involve yourself with his reading abilities. Reading is only one aspect of using languages, and while he is still quite young, a baby even, you can help him by talking to him constantly. As he gets older take time to listen to him and allow him to ask endless questions, however repetitive and absurd. Research has shown that children who talk a lot, and who have learnt a wide vocabulary in chatting with their parents, don't usually have trouble with reading.

Later on, when he starts to read at school, listen to him reading a little bit every day, and show him that you enjoy books too by reading regularly to him, probably at bedtime.

There are many methods of teaching reading in the primary schools today. Some depend on a special alphabet like 'ita', the initial teaching alphabet, which aims to sort out the difficulties of English spelling and pronunciation. Others depend on colour coding, or systems of 'phonetics'. The 'Breakthrough to Literacy' scheme combines the teaching of reading with writing at a very early stage. Most teachers are only too glad to explain to parents the method which they operate in their schools.

Most infant school heads aim for the children to be able to read by the time they go up to the junior school. If your child is still not reading by the age of seven, don't despair. But do speak to the junior head teacher and find out if there is anything you can usefully do at home, and what arrangements are being made to help him. Above all don't be panicked into arranging private coaching. For this may only confuse the child. Play it all as lightly as possible. Don't let your child think of reading as a tedious and fearsome chore. But show by your own example, if you can, that it is a useful delight.

It would be foolish to state an exact age at which you should expect a child to read. Some pretty average children seem to pick up the skill very quickly, almost without any greater source of pride than the ability to do a backward somersault.

There are records of some extremely clever people who didn't read until a late age. On the whole, though, most teachers are agreed that if a child is not reading fairly fluently by the time he enters the junior school, then his progress needs to be watched very carefully.

Further information: Donald Moyle, *The Teaching of Reading*, Ward Lock Educational, 1968. Vera Southgate and G. R. Roberts, *Reading – Which Approach?*, University of London Press, 1970. Pamela McKeown, *Reading – a basic guide for Parents and Teachers*, Routledge & Kegan Paul, 1974.

Recognition as Efficient

'Recognition as efficient' has no legal status. It is a mark of approval from the Department of Education for which independent schools can apply if they want.

To be recognized, schools must be inspected by HM INSPECTORS, as they are for REGISTRATION. But this time the standards applied are a little bit stricter.

The standards for recognition are set out in a strange document known as 'Rules 16' (from the DES), which says that besides complying with the four criteria of registration, the school must provide a 'progressive general education' (whatever that means) and have a state school level of efficiency. Some state schools don't themselves come up to this standard.

See also SCHOOLS, LISTS OF.

Registered Schools

Don't be taken in by schools which advertise themselves as 'Registered with the Department of Education'. All private – that is independent – schools in England and Wales have to be registered, so the claim doesn't mean anything. The law only asks the DES to be satisfied as to the 'suitability' and 'adequacy' of the buildings, the 'efficiency and suitability' of the instruction, and the 'properness' of the staff. Clearly, almost anything is possible under these headings. And schools are given plenty of time to put their houses in order.

You would be well advised to ask why – unless the school is less than two years old – it has not applied for RECOGNIZED status. Unless it is an unusual school with aims that are outside traditional school practice, the fact that it has achieved only registration could be disturbing.

Religious Education

All state schools must give religious education by law. It's the only school subject that's legally compulsory.

You have the right to withdraw your child from lessons on religion if you are against his being taught it, or if you want him to have denominational teaching instead. The local education authority (through the head teacher) has legal power to make arrangements for him to be taught his own religion outside the school, so long as this doesn't interfere with the rest of his work. This means in practice that it can happen only at the beginning or end of the school day.

Such special arrangements can still be very inconvenient for everyone, including the child concerned. So the local authority will make them only if it can't find a school for the child to go to as a regular pupil which gives the kind of religious teaching you want.

Supposing you are a Catholic and want your boy or girl to have Catholic teaching, but you think the local Catholic school is a bad one, you might think you could send them to the local county school and have them 'withdrawn' to the Catholic school. But here you'll have quite a tussle and the law won't help you at all. The scheme would work only if the Catholic school were too full to take your child in the first place.

The law was drawn up in 1944 and doesn't say that the religious teaching has got to be Christian – it merely assumes it will be. The 1944 Act provides for 'agreed syllabuses' to be drawn up by representatives of the authorities and the churches. These syllabuses used to be based very much on Bible history and Bible stories but the later editions are concerned much more with moral questions as the starting point, bringing in the Christian teaching to help solve them. The Church of England in particular believes much more in the 'soft sell' these days.

A lot of religious instruction is hardly religious at all. It's really 'moral education', with pupils discussing what they'd do in difficult family situations, for example. In schools where more than half the pupils aren't Christian, the 1944 Act and the agreed syllabuses are not much help in any case.

Further information: Kathleen Gibberd, *Teaching Religion in Schools*, Longmans, 1970. *The Fourth R*, Society for the Promotion of Christian Knowledge, 1970 (report of an independent committee under the Bishop of Durham). For the case against compulsory religious education, contact the National Secular Society, 103 Borough High Street, London SE1.

Remedial Classes. See BACKWARDNESS; SPECIAL SCHOOLS.

Reports

School reports may come termly or yearly; they may be full and detailed, or laconic and brief. Parents have no right to demand that they should take any particular form or even that there should be a written report at all. But a school which didn't somehow keep parents informed about their children's progress could be breaking the law which requires them to consult with parents (Section 76 of the 1944 Education Act).

How much notice should be taken of a bad report – or, for that matter, of a good one? It is worth remembering that writers of reports face two temptations: (1) To play down pupils' achievements so as to make them work harder next term (a common technique among schools which rely on exam results to attract custom); and (2) to overpraise their work so as to show that the school is doing its job.

Again, a teacher may report that a child is stupid to excuse his own shortcomings.

A minority of teachers believe that all reports should always be encouraging. Their remarks may be unreliable, but at least they're on the side of the child.

Unless they clearly fall into the last category, there's little to be said for showing children their reports. The only reliable information is the marks and form order, which they will probably know already. Many schools, deplorably, save money by sending the report home via the child, with instructions to the child not to open it: the worst possible way, arousing curiosity yet implying secrecy.

If you think a report is unfair it is important to query it, because it may go on file as part of a pupil's CONFIDENTIAL RECORD. Space for parents to sign in and add their comments is usually much too small, but you can always attach a sheet.

For example: the report says: 'Arithmetic: only fair. Must learn to listen.' Your reply: 'I see that Jane seems to have lost interest in arithmetic. She was all right under her last teacher and we were wondering what the trouble was.' A blustering

108   *Reports*

tone doesn't help; it will merely mark you down as nuisance parents.

Reports on school leavers for the youth employment service can by law be seen by parents; but they are not the parents' property and can't be taken away. The parent has no right to a copy.

Further information: Leslie Keating, *The School Report*, Kenneth Mason, 13–14 Homewell, Havant, Hants, 1969.

Retarded. See BACKWARDNESS.

Rules

A parent who sends a child to school is presumed, under common law, to have given the teachers the power to make rules for the child (see our note on *in loco parentis*, page x). These include rules which affect the good order of the school both inside *and* outside the school premises. So if you do have a choice of school it's wise to find out what the rules are first, since there won't be much that can be done about them once your child is at school. This applies to all schools, whether state or private.

But the law also says the rules should be 'reasonable', and in fact heads usually make sure they are known to parents. The one thing they don't want is a demo on their hands. The National Union of Teachers' *Handbook of School Administration* says: 'The active co-operation of the parents should be sought and maintained at all times.'

If you are annoyed about a silly rule there's little point in appealing to managers, governors or the local education office: they will leave these matters to the discretion of the head teacher. But if enough parents kick up a fuss and complain that he's being unreasonable, there'll be a strong chance that he will change his mind.

Scholastic Agencies

These give free advice on choice of private schools, tutors, coaching establishments, secretarial courses and so forth. The more precise you are about what you want, the more they'll help. Bear in mind, though, that they take commission from the schools. Best-known: Gabbitas-Thring Educational Trust, 6–8 Sackville Street, London W1; Truman and Knightley Educational Trust, 78 Notting Hill Gate, London W11.

School Bus. See TRANSPORT.

School Councils

School Councils are the result of the obvious idea that the consumers of the school system should have some say in its organization. At least you might think it was obvious, but not every head teacher does.

The late A. S. Neill, founder of Summerhill School, decided from the beginning to have a weekly meeting of all pupils and staff at which everyone had an equal, single vote, including the head master. A growing number of secondary schools have a watered-down version of this system.

In many of them it is a sop to the first murmurings of discontent among pupils (see PUPIL POWER). But generally the head keeps his hand firmly on the reins. He has the final veto on all decisions of the council, except perhaps over harmless areas like choice of school meals.

It's not only the pupils who welcome the idea of the school council. In some schools the junior staff complain that they are consulted even less than the pupils.

If you believe that your children can learn the true meaning of democracy only by practising it, you have a duty to encourage some real democracy in their schools.

Further information: Little Red School Book, Stage 1, 21 Theobalds Road, London WC1.

School Fund

There are all sorts of incidental expenses that crop up in running a school which are not covered by official funds. A teacher may need some particular piece of equipment that is out of the usual run of educational supplies. There may be prizes to be bought for sports days or speech days. Kit for the school football and cricket teams may not be provided by the local authority. There may be extra expenses in connection with away games or school journeys.

Most schools cope with these items by having a school fund, sometimes asking children to make a weekly contribution. It isn't compulsory to make such contributions, and you shouldn't be bullied into it if you can't pay. But school funds are a harmless and useful way of helping the school along.

Other ways of swelling school funds include fêtes and garden parties, the sale of crisps or fruit at breaktime, donations from parent–teacher associations, and (a very common way) commission on school photographs.

There's no need to fear that school funds are spent in unauthorized ways. Local authorities lay down rules about the management of them. One invariable rule is that they should not be spent on educational supplies which would normally be paid for out of official money.

School Journeys

Day trips during term-time are paid for by the school, so all you need to provide is a little pocket-money or whatever food the teacher says your child should take. No teacher should be in charge of more than fifteen pupils. More than that is not safe, and if you find your child is going on parties bigger than this, under only one teacher, you should take the matter up with the head. Walking or climbing trips often have stricter conditions.

Holiday trips at home and abroad are generally not paid for and it's up to you to decide whether the child should go. The pressure will be strong and many parents worry whether it's worth the expense.

If there is a choice between home trips and trips abroad and your child is of primary school age, the home trip might well be

School Journeys 111

the better bet, apart from being cheaper. Too many teachers assume that there's some point in going abroad just for the sake of it.

A clue might be found in the travel agency handling the trip. There are plenty of agencies willing to cash in on the fashion for foreign travel by advertising 'educational tours' which have nothing specially educational about them. See below for how to identify the respectable ones.

If the cost looks altogether too much (and it could be as much as £100 for a foreign trip), it's worth asking whether there are any arrangements for subsidizing it, say through the SCHOOL FUND.

Exchange visits are probably the best way of getting abroad for young people – and they're the cheapest, if you decide to be host to another child from abroad. One-to-one exchanges are likely to be a better bet than the many language schools. Such exchanges mean that your child is likely to be well treated by the foreign family, and he'll certainly learn the language faster.

You could make your first contact with a foreign family either through the modern languages department at school or through an organization specializing in exchanges (see below).

You should check whether your child will be accompanied by an adult on his journeyings, and whether the agency has an employee living in the country in question, who can be turned to in times of crisis, if any. And, when your child's 'exchange' comes to stay with you, treat him as you hope his parents treated yours.

Finding an agency is not difficult. Ask your child's teachers, or write for information to the Government-financed Central Bureau for Educational Visits and Exchanges. Its address is: 43 Dorset Street, London W1H 3FN.

Further information: The Central Bureau for Educational Visits and Exchanges, *Youth and student travel*; *Vacation courses abroad*; *Working holidays abroad*; *School travel and exchange* (latest editions). *The Education Committees Year Book* (latest edition – the chapter on educational travel), Councils and Education Press (see ADVICE).

School Magazines

An important shop window for any school, the magazine is generally under the close control of head or a member of the staff. The school has the copyright of anything that appears in it, including that lovely poem your daughter wrote for it. In independent schools, often an unavoidable EXTRA.

Schools, Lists of

Every state secondary school in the United Kingdom is listed in the *Education Committees Year Book* (see ADVICE).

There is no similar list for primary schools. For them you will have to ask the local education office, also listed.

Some local authorities are, meanwhile, very reluctant to disclose names of governors or managers. But since the *Year Book* names the chief education officer, staff and all the education committee, you know where to make a fuss if necessary.

Independent schools are listed geographically in the annual publication called *Schools*, published by Truman and Knightley. Independent schools RECOGNIZED AS EFFICIENT are in the official *List of Independent Schools in England and Wales*, otherwise called 'List 70' (HMSO). It gives names of owners and heads, numbers and sex of pupils, whether boarding or not, and FEES.

Public schools (HMC SCHOOLS) are detailed in *The Public and Preparatory Schools Year Book* (A. & C. Black, annually). The PREPARATORY SCHOOLS in this book are only those belonging to the Incorporated Association of Preparatory Schools. For the GIRLS' SCHOOLS, there is the companion volume, the *Girls' School Year Book*. A. & C. Black also do an *Independent Schools Association Year Book*.

Secondary Schools

Schools for people between eleven and nineteen. GRAMMAR SCHOOLS and COMPREHENSIVE SCHOOLS are secondary schools. So are secondary modern schools, though hardly anyone uses that expression these days. It means secondary schools which

Secretary of State for Education and Science

take only those children who are not supposed to be clever enough to get into a grammar school, where one exists. Nowadays they're usually called just 'secondary' or 'county secondary'. For variations on the system, see also MIDDLE SCHOOLS.

Secretary of State for Education and Science

The Secretary of State for Education and Science is the minister responsible to Parliament for the operation of the education system.

Although the Secretary of State is the 'boss' of the education system, he doesn't expect to be troubled with trifling complaints about particular children. Parents have the right to appeal direct to the Secretary of State, but it's normally more useful to keep that right in reserve as a last resort. In any case, if you do write to the Secretary of State, he will merely make inquiries of the LOCAL EDUCATION AUTHORITY and repeat its answer in a letter to you. The truth of the matter is that the Education Act lays down the principles, the Secretary of State oversees them, and the local authorities are responsible for carrying them out in detail.

All the same, the possibility of an appeal to the Secretary of State on an issue of real importance (that is, perhaps on the allocation of your child to a particular secondary school, not because he was made to change for games on a cold day) is worth keeping in mind. If you do write, make sure that you have the facts at your fingertips and concentrate on facts, not colourful detail. The Department's address is Elizabeth House, York Road, London SE1.

Further information: William Alexander, *Education in England* (2nd edn), Ginn, 1970.

Selection. See ELEVEN-PLUS.

Sex Education

Today's parents are often worried about the way their children may come to learn about sex and related topics. Today's children still learn a certain amount from friends at school. But added to this uncertain source is one which was hardly available to their parents at their age. The Press and television programmes of all kinds, not just schools television, offer information about childbirth, contraception, homosexuality, venereal disease, subjects which are taken in by children in a way that is neither surreptitious nor unhealthy.

But information gathered in this way, often by a chance reference in a discussion programme or in a news item, can be misunderstood or misinterpreted. For this reason more and more schools have come to recognize that they have a duty to supplement such information with facts and rational discussion, carefully presented and planned.

Often it starts in the primary school, and it's as well that it does. Before puberty children show the same intense and healthy interest in the process of reproduction and other bodily functions like excretion as they do about how the eye sees or the ear hears; at least they do as long as they haven't been induced by parents or other well-meaning adults to think that any reference to sex or excretion is taboo, or worse still, 'dirty'.

Children in secondary schools find it easier to approach the problems of sex openly if they've already learnt the facts a few years before. But they, too, want knowledge about sex. They may have forgotten what they once learned, and even if they think they know everything already, tragic mistakes can be avoided by learning at this stage the odd fact which they didn't know they didn't know.

At this age, information needs to be linked with discussion about relationships, about rights and duties, about right and wrong. This will mean talking openly and perhaps forming opinions about contraception, abortion, living together before marriage.

Sometimes teachers excuse themselves from taking such discussions, and the school invites an outsider to come and do it, someone like a marriage guidance counsellor, the school medical officer or even a parson. But today teachers of all ages feel less distant from their pupils than they used to do, and it may well be better both for them and for the children if they do the talking themselves. In this way, the whole business becomes less formal, and less special.

The Department of Education has no policy on sex education. It takes its usual line that what's taught in the schools (apart from religious knowledge) is none of its business. The result is what you'd expect: tremendous variations between area and area and even between schools in the same area.

Some schools bring the subject into health education or even 'civics', some into biology, using the many textbooks available. The books are seldom adequate, though. They tend to waver uncertainly between the too-clinical and the too-sentimental approach.

Classroom discussion often leads to children starting discussions on these matters openly with their parents. Many parents welcome this. Some parents are apprehensive that sex officially dealt with in school may put indesirable thoughts into their children's minds (they seem to disregard what goes in unofficially via other children).

It is, of course, possible to ask for a child to be excluded from specific lessons, and unlikely that the request will be turned down. But it should be this way round. The changes in attitude to sex have now reached the schools; most of them seem to deal with the matter and they deal with it responsibly. They shouldn't feel obliged to send a note to parents, as they once did, 'warning' them that the dreaded topic was going to be dealt with.

Further information: The Health Education Council, 78 New Oxford Street, London WC1A 1AH, produces a free duplicated guide to publications and teaching aids on sex education. The Family Planning Association, 27–35 Mortimer Street, London W1A 40W, produces a free booklist which includes a section on this subject.

Single-sex Schools

Teachers and parents who believe in single-sex education say school-children – and especially adolescents – learn a lot of things better when the sexes are segregated. Boys and girls develop at different rates, so what interests the one may leave the other bored or bewildered.

Again, both sexes may be distracted by the need to impress each other. There is, too, the danger that girls in a co-ed may shy away from supposedly 'masculine' subjects like maths or science.

Before making up one's mind, though, it's well to give some thought to the case for CO-EDUCATION.

The argument on both sides naturally gets fiercer when it comes to boarding education. People who believe in keeping boys and girls apart say contradictory things: that having them together is dangerous for their morals (not proven!) – and that segregation doesn't matter too much anyway because boys and girls have plenty of chances to meet outside school.

Another point. Girls interested in maths and science may find they don't get so many good specialist teachers in girls' schools. Watch for this if you're thinking of an independent school for your daughter. Independent girls' boarding schools can be very petty in their rules, giving little freedom. (Which, let's admit it, is why lots of parents like them.)

Further information: R. R. Dale, *Mixed or Single-Sex Schools* (3 vols.), Routledge & Kegan Paul, 1965, 1967 and 1974. A very full research study. Kathleen Ollerenshaw, *The Girls' Schools*, Faber, 1967. Deals only with independent schools.

Sixth-form Colleges

These are for sixteen-to-nineteen-year-olds. By 1974 nearly seventy of them were built or planned, avoiding huge comprehensive schools for the eleven-to-eighteen age group. Few have any conditions of entry.

Their attraction and advantage is that they have a more adult atmosphere than ordinary sixth forms. But they vary a

Special Schools 117

lot in their rules. Some are like big boys' grammar schools, others more like technical colleges.

Further information: The Sixth Form College in Practice, Councils and Education Press, 1972. Rupert Wearing King, *The English Sixth Form College*, Pergamon, 1968. *Comprehensive Education*, numbers 20 and 21, 1972, Campaign for Comprehensive Education (see ADVICE).

Slow Learners. See BACKWARDNESS; SPECIAL SCHOOLS.

Smoking, Drinking

A pupil who smokes or drinks on the way to or from school or during the lunch hour, even if outside the school gates, could still be breaking a school rule.

Some secondary schools allow smoking and drinking among sixth-formers at certain times and in certain places. It's all part of the movement to give older pupils more personal responsibility for the way they organize their own lives.

Further information: The Young Smoker, HMSO, 1969. A report of the Government Social Survey.

Spastic Children. See SPECIAL SCHOOLS.

Special schools

Children with any mental or physical handicap, such as BACKWARDNESS, severe emotional problems, DEAFNESS, blindness or any of the various forms of spasticity are entitled to special education. This means that they will attend institutions specially suited to their needs, where the teachers are trained to help them to minimize their handicaps and to live as fully as possible. All children, however severely handicapped, come under the responsibility of the LOCAL EDUCATION AUTHORITIES and all are entitled to whatever education they can benefit from, and to the attention of a trained teacher. Most special schools deal with a particular range of handicap so that you will not expect to find children with severe physical handicaps such as blindness or cerebral palsy in a school for the EDUCATIONALLY SUBNORMAL.

It is becoming increasingly common for children with physical handicaps (some of such severity as to demand confinement to a wheelchair) to be provided for in ordinary schools. But this still means that special arrangements will have to be made. When a handicap is so severe, as in the case of blindness or extensive maladjustment, that a boarding school is felt to be the best solution, local authorities can make arrangements for fees to be paid to institutions outside their area if need be. If this happens you are entitled to claim towards your travelling expenses to visit the child. It is very important that children in boarding schools realize that they are still part of the family.

A pupil may only be withdrawn from a special school with the consent of the local education authority. If your child is a pupil in a special school and you feel that, for one reason or another, he should now attend an ordinary school, you have the right of referral to the Secretary of State for Education. Your child will have been placed in the special school, after the local authority's medical officer has issued a certificate to say that he is suffering from such a mental or physical handicap that he needs special schooling. There is no legal provision for a second medical opinion in this matter, but if a case is referred to the Department of Education and Science, it is allowable for the child to be seen by one of the department's doctors.

There is no doubt that the sooner a handicap is diagnosed the better. This responsibility often falls on the parents. Living with the child every day, they are the ones who notice if he is not developing as well as his brothers or sisters or the other children in the neighbourhood. If your child's teacher complains that he is not keeping up with his class, it may be because he can't hear or see properly. If you suspect that this is the case and that your child's hearing or eyesight is below average, consult your GP. He will put you on to the school medical service if he feels that education in a special school is required. In most cases that will not be necessary.

Special schools also cater for delicate or asthmatic children, who need periods of rest during the day, long periods in the open air and possibly special diets. As these handicaps are usually curable, a delicate child may only need to spend a year or two of his education in a special school of this nature.

Further information: Barbara Furneaux, *The Special Child*, Penguin, 1969.
Useful organizations: National Association for Mentally Handicapped Children, Pembridge Hall, 17 Pembridge Square, London W2. Invalid Children's Aid Association, 126 Buckingham Palace Road, London SW1W 9SB. National Children's Bureau (see ADVICE). Spastics Society, 12 Park Crescent, London W1N 4EQ.

Speech Day

Annual prizegiving with a distinguished speaker and head's report. The important thing it lacks is an exchange of views. It's a one-way system, and this is not the best way of teaching. Heads are gradually persuading governors to give it up, and use other occasions for getting parents or employers together, or getting space in the local press.

Spelling

Spelling is something everyone gets worked up about. If you can spell, you tend to think that everyone else should spell as well as you; if you can't, you worry about it.

In fact, spelling is important, but not all *that* important. There are plenty of distinguished people whose spelling is hopeless, and equally there are plenty of undistinguished people who spell perfectly. The old way of teaching spelling was to learn five or ten words a day, but there is no evidence that most children remembered them once they'd had their 'spelling test'. And this method also led to lots of children learning words like 'eucalyptus' and 'anthropomorphic' which they probably never used again in their lives. These days, good teachers tend to teach spelling as words come up in conversation or writing, and they encourage children to use dictionaries when they're in doubt.

There are three ways parents can help with spelling, all of them very simple. First, no home should be without a good dictionary. Second, parents should do all they can to encourage their children to read widely. Third, children's failures in spelling should be accepted sympathetically; the correct spellings could be pointed out, rather than emphasis being placed on the mistakes.

Further information: M. L. Peters, *Spelling: Caught or Taught?*, Routledge & Kegan Paul, 1967.

Starting School

The exact age your child will start at INFANT SCHOOL very much depends on the town in which you live. Although many infant heads would like to take all the new children in at the beginning of the school year in September, this is rarely practical. Some arrange two intakes a year (September and April). Others take children in throughout the year as soon as each individual turns five. Usually some arrangement is devised which falls between the extremes. Although five is the compulsory school starting age, a certain amount of flexibility is allowed, and more and more infant schools are arranging to take in four-year-olds at the beginning of the term in which they become five.

For a four- or five-year-old, who has spent all his life at home with his mother, the first day at school can be a shattering experience. Most infant head teachers are aware of this, and make arrangements for children to visit the school frequently before they start full-time attendance. Some will even be able to allow them to come into school one afternoon a week during the term before they start, and for their mothers to stay with them if they seem in any way upset. Do take advantage of this arrangement. It means that when your child comes to start school he will be entering a familiar building where at least some of the people are known to him.

Some infant schools are now taking in children long before their fifth birthday and although this can be good in many ways there can be drawbacks and parents should be aware of them. It's not wise to withdraw a child from a good NURSERY SCHOOL when he is four years old because he has been offered a place in the infant school. At present many excellent infant school teachers do not have the training or experience to work with children below the age of five. If you do decide to send your child to infant school at four, you are not compelled by law to see that he attends both morning and afternoon sessions until he becomes five. So have a word with the head teacher about HALF-TIME SCHOOLING. She can arrange this at her discretion.

Further information: M. Chazan, A. Laing and S. Jackson, *Just before school*, Oxford University Press, 1971. R. Palmer, *Starting School*, University of London Press, 1971. Mary C. Churchill, 'First term coming up', *Nursery World*, 3 May 1973.

State Schools

Means all schools maintained by LOCAL EDUCATION AUTHORITIES. Sometimes also called maintained schools. If they're county schools, they were founded by, and are owned by, the authorities. If they're voluntary schools, they were founded by religious bodies (see CHURCH SCHOOLS). All state schools are free.

Stealing. See DELINQUENCY.

Streaming

This means putting pupils in different classes according to their ability. It can happen as early as seven years old. The result is that the child is typecast as bright or not-so-bright from then on, and gets treated accordingly. People who believe in streaming can claim that it works, because the pupils in the top streams do better than those in the lower streams, and this shows they were put in the right places to start with. This is a false argument, because it's well known that pupils tend to rise or sink to the level of their classmates, so it's nothing more than a self-fulfilling prophecy.

Streaming is common throughout the education system. Theoretically a child can be transferred to a higher stream if he does well. But this doesn't often happen, for the reason already given. Many comprehensive schools don't stream for the first two or three years, but wait for the pupils to sort themselves out by their own preferences before separating them into academic and non-academic classes.

A recent Government-supported survey into the whole question concluded that children's success in school depended less on whether they were formally streamed than on what their teachers thought of them.

'Banding' is a variant of streaming. It means that there are several classes of roughly the same ability in each band. It can be found in some very big comprehensive schools.

'Setting' means that although a class is not streamed it breaks up into other groups for certain subjects, such as maths and modern languages, in which it's said that it's difficult to teach pupils of widely differing attainments. Even very progressive countries such as Sweden, which disbelieve in streaming, use setting.

Whether a school is streamed or not is one of the questions worth asking when it comes to choice of school. There are good streamed schools and bad unstreamed ones.

You should be wary of a primary school which streams carefully so as to make sure it gives the cream of its teaching to those likely to pass the eleven-plus.

Further information: Joan C. Barker Lunn, *Streaming in the Primary School*, National Foundation for Educational Research, 1970, particularly the section of conclusions.

Strikes. See PARENTS' RIGHTS.

Subjects

It is generally thought nowadays that if a child wants to take a certain subject he ought to be allowed to do so, if there is someone to teach it. Things have changed a lot here. In the not-so-old days subject teachers would be able to say: 'I'm not taking her, she's too dim.'

In primary schools and at the bottom of secondary schools where everyone does a common course there's naturally not much choice anyway. Problems do arise when pupils begin to specialize. A subject may be refused, not because the school thinks the pupil is unsuitable for it, but because the timetable isn't flexible enough.

A sensible secondary school will allow pupils to take subjects in the local technical college if the school itself can't provide them. The pupils are 'farmed out' for, say, an afternoon a week.

For more advice on this topic, see EXAMINATIONS.

The only subject which is compulsory by law in state schools is religion. The state schools make their own rules about what other subjects are compulsory and parents are expected to comply.

If a parent wanted to push a child into a certain subject and the child clearly didn't want to do it, the likelihood is that the school would side with the pupil.

Suspension. See EXPULSION.

Tax Concessions. See FEES.

Teachers

Teachers are a very well-organized profession and nearly always close ranks when any one of them is attacked. It's a point of professional etiquette with them not to criticize each other personally in front of non-teachers. If one teacher wants to make a complaint against another there are elaborate procedures for dealing with it.

It's practically impossible to get a bad teacher sacked, unless

124   *Teachers*

a criminal act is involved. Heads have been known to give good references to unsatisfactory or incompetent members of staff just to get rid of them. For advice about what to do if you think a teacher is behaving badly, see ASSAULT and COMPLAINTS.

Some old-fashioned teachers, believe it or not, think it's bad practice to visit the homes of pupils. Some parents admittedly wouldn't want a visit from a teacher. Luckily such ideas are gradually breaking down. Meanwhile it would be wrong to feel too hurt if you found a class teacher surprisingly stuffy or off-putting. It could just be the result of a sort of professional inferiority complex. In any case, it's wise to approach teachers fairly formally, until you know them. They like it that way. For example, a note to say you want to see a teacher (rather than just turning up) is appreciated.

There is no sure way of telling a good teacher from a bad one (leaving aside the minority who so obviously hate children!) Some amazingly pompous ones turn out to be marvellous in class.

Further information: There's an enormous literature about teachers, but for a brief account of how they see themselves see Tony Gibson, *Teachers Talking*, Allen Lane, 1973.

Team-teaching

In team-teaching, a number of teachers combine to take charge of two or more classes, working out an agreed course of lessons which cuts across the usual subject barriers. It might, for instance, be a project covering various aspects of English, history and geography. Sometimes all the classes might join together for a film shown by the geography teacher; sometimes a class might split into two, one being taught by the English specialist, another by the historian, and so forth. Yes, it works – if the teachers get on together!

A not-so-good kind is where there might be, for example, two infant teachers, one well-qualified, the other not. So two adjacent infant classes are combined. The experienced teacher skips from one class to another while the other minds the children. That is not proper team-teaching, though it might be called by the name.

Technical Colleges. See COLLEGES OF FURTHER EDUCATION.

Textbooks

These days, teachers don't see their job as passing on slabs of pre-digested knowledge. So the old-style textbook, through which a class worked more or less at the same time, has almost disappeared.

Modern books for schools are more 'open-ended' – that is, they provide information and suggest rather than dictate things for the children to do. Even in examination courses, today's children have a good deal of choice in what topics they follow up.

In many schools, children learn from materials which are not in book form at all. Subjects such as mathematics, junior science and history are often taught with kits of cards, which may provide information as well as suggest different items of work. The cards are sometimes backed up with films, film-strips, tape-recordings or discs.

Also found in increasing numbers in schools are books of the sort you would see in the children's section of the public library – well-produced information books on all manner of subjects from astronomy to zoology. Pupils use these as sources when they produce their own work.

Transport

If a child under eight lives more than two miles from school, the local authority *must* provide transport to and fro; for children over eight, the distance is three miles. What kind of transport it provides is up to the local authority. It can give free passes on service buses, it can send round a school bus, or it can even send a taxi round to call for each child – and many local authorities in remote areas do just that.

All sorts of problems arise over transport to and from school. First, there's the question of timing. If a school bus is going round the countryside picking up odd children here and there, it may arrive at your house ridiculously early. But there it is, one of the penalties to set against the pleasures of living in a remote spot. Then, of course, there are the border-line cases – the child of eight who's just under the two-mile limit but may still have to walk along a dangerous lane.

On the whole, local authorities are sensible about these things, and often bend the rule a little to take in border-line cases. But they have their costs to work out, and they can only bend the rules so far. If you're in a border-line area, it's always worth trying to see if you can get your child on the school bus. But it's best not to approach the local authority in a spirit of fuming against red tape. Where school buses are run, it's more likely that they will stop for you than it is that you will be able to persuade the local authority to part with a free pass for a service bus. As always in cases of COMPLAINTS or appeals, get your facts right. Just *how* far is it from your gate to the school?

Truancy

'Truant' is a blanket term used to describe anyone who is absent from school without a 'good reason' (i.e. an easily understood one like illness, bereavement, etc.). Rising truancy rates in inner city areas are taken to be one of the symptoms of a growing crisis in education. Many in the education service like to explain truancy entirely in terms of reasons internal to the child (school phobia, unhappiness at home, maladjustment, etc.). It is hardly ever seen as a legitimate protest against a barbarous, insensitive or irrelevant school situation.

If you find that your child is playing truant, do not be too quick to assume that it is his fault, or that the only solution is to force him back to school. The child may have a reasonable explanation, and one worth taking up with the school. He may have some very positive and useful ideas about the sort of education he needs, too.

If you take a hard-line attitude which makes it impossible for the child to discuss truancy with you, it is likely that he will resort to further deception, and it is at that stage that the link between truancy and some forms of DELINQUENCY becomes apparent. See also ATTENDANCE and ABSENCE.

Tuition Fees. See FEES.

Tutors. See COACHING AND CRAMMING.

Uniforms
There is no law which says school-children should wear uniform. But if the head insists on it there is nothing you can do.

However, if your income is below a certain level you may be eligible for a GRANT towards the cost from your local education welfare office, which is part of the LOCAL EDUCATION AUTHORITY. If you don't know where to apply the head teacher will tell you, or write to the LEA for you. The grant may take the form of a voucher for use at a particular shop. Some welfare offices keep their own stocks.

Until recently it has been the practice in most areas to give grants only for uniform, not for general clothing. But as more and more schools drop the requirement for children to wear a set uniform, it is becoming more common for families to get help with clothing in general. You should certainly be ready to argue with a welfare office which says that the money is only available for set uniforms.

To qualify for help with uniform your income does have to be very low. There is no set level for the country as a whole, and individual offices have a great deal of discretion. As with other benefits, they may want to know a lot about your circumstances – what rent you pay, how many dependants you have etc., before making a decision.

Only if you are already getting supplementary benefit can you be really sure of being eligible for a uniform grant. Nor have you an actual right to a grant. Some local authorities are very mean, some generous. A recent test case at Greenhithe, Kent, was helpful. A supplementary benefits tribunal ruled that

128   *Uniforms*

a certain family living on supplementary benefit should have a grant for the whole cost of the child's uniform.

The argument in favour of uniforms is that children whose parents are too poor to have nice clothes won't stick out like sore thumbs at school. The argument falls down when the uniform is so elaborate that the poor families can't afford it and the local authority is mean over grants. Other countries get by quite nicely without school uniforms.

In Britain more and more schools are seeing sense and making uniforms simpler or doing without them altogether.

See also EQUIPMENT; EXTRAS; PERSONAL APPEARANCE.

Further information: Where on Parents and Law, ACE (see ADVICE), has a section on how far a school or LEA can enforce the wearing of a school uniform.

Universities

Universities are thought by most people to be the aristocrats of the education system and getting to one is believed to be the best thing that could happen to an eighteen-year-old. Not necessarily, though.

A university degree doesn't guarantee a job. It doesn't guarantee wisdom either. A man can go right through university and still be a fool at the end of it.

Would-be applicants with fewer than two A-levels in the GCE should look elsewhere for their higher education (see DEGREES). Obviously, an applicant with three or more high-grade A-levels stands a better chance than someone with two low-grade ones.

The first step towards getting into university is for your child to decide which course he wants to study, which university to study at, and why he wants to go. A teacher's advice should be sought as early as possible.

Applications to all but a very few universities are made through the clearing-house organization known as the Universities Central Council on Admissions (address: PO Box 28, Cheltenham, Gloucestershire GL50 1HY). The school should provide an UCCA application form and the all-important handbook that shows how to fill the form in.

The handbook will, among other things, tell the candidate to list on his form the five universities he would be interested in going to, in order of preference if he wishes. He can name fewer – but his chances of success increase with the number of alternatives he offers.

Unless it's absolutely essential, and however carefully he – and you – have checked the handbook through, he should not fill in his form without a teacher's help. A teacher (usually the head) or another referee has to complete a section of it, and it is the referee who is responsible for sending the form back to UCCA.

Forms must be submitted by 15 December. For Oxford and Cambridge, the last date is 15 November. (The university year begins in October.) That means you're applying before the results of A-level are known.

UCCA cheeringly points out that at least two-thirds of the UK candidates for university places are successful the first or second time round, provided they have the minimum qualifications. But it also stresses that applicants should make alternative plans, to be put into operation if they can't get a university place. In this connection, see POLYTECHNICS and COLLEGES OF FURTHER EDUCATION.

Further information: Which University?, Haymarket Press, annually. *Choosing a University*, ACE (see ADVICE).

Vandalism. See DELINQUENCY.

Vertical Grouping. See FAMILY GROUPING.

Violence. See ASSAULT; DELINQUENCY.

Voluntary Schools. See CHURCH SCHOOLS.

Welfare Benefits

Various kinds of assistance are available to low-income families. The best known is free school meals. In most areas, forms setting out the details and explaining how to apply are circulated to every family, usually through the school. The application forms are absurdly long and complicated. If you are in any doubt about how to apply, whether you are eligible, whether you have been wrongly turned down, etc., get advice either from your local education office or education welfare office (usually the same place) or through a Citizens Advice Bureau, local branch of the Child Poverty Action Group (see below), etc.

For children staying at school beyond the leaving age (sixteen) there are maintenance GRANTS. And in certain cases help is available towards the cost of school UNIFORMS and other clothing, holidays, books, etc. If you feel you really need help, it is well worthwhile talking perhaps first to a sympathetic teacher, and then to your local education welfare office or social services department.

See also ADVICE.

Useful organizations: Child Poverty Action Group (has local branches); headquarters: see ADVICE. Also Citizen's Rights Office at same address. Citizen's Advice Bureaux: over 500 round the country; headquarters at 26 Bedford Square, London WC1.

Zoning. See CATCHMENT AREA.